<<神秘的塔里木>>編委會

編委會主任: 李康寧

編委會成員: 邵　强　郭衛民　柴庚存
　　　　　　陳宏博　池重慶　尼　相
　　　　　　張遇良　陳重秋

主　　　編: 張遇良　陳宏博

執 行 主編: 梁　楓

副　主　編: 武純展　巴赫提亞　張　田

總 體 設計: 梁　楓　武純展

文 字 編輯: 姜新建

撰　　　文: 武純展

英　　　譯: 孫錦雲

責 任 編輯: 梁　楓

攝　　　影: 武純展　梁　楓

（其中: "營盤"、"安迪尔"、"丹丹乌里克"、"楼兰"、"尼雅"部分）

撰　　　文: 肖小勇　阮秋榮　李文瑛

英　　　譯: 肖小勇

編　　　輯: 劉玉生

攝　　　影: 劉玉生

Director of the Editorial Committee:Li Kangning

Members of the Editorial Committee:Shao Qiang　Guo Weimin　Chai Gengcun
　　　　　　　　　　　　　　　　　　Chen Hongbo　Chi Chongqing　Nixiang
　　　　　　　　　　　　　　　　　　Zhang Yuliang　Chen Zhongqiu

Chief Editors:Zhang Yuliang　Chen Hongbo

Deputy Editors:Bahtiyar　zhang Tian　Wu Chunzhan

Executine Editor:Liang Feng

General Designer:Liang Feng

Editor:Jiang Xinjian

Executive editor:Liang Feng

Writers:Wu Chunzhan

English Translation:Sun Jinyun

Photography:wu Chunzhan　Liang Feng

(The part of "Ying Pan"、"Endere"、"Dandan -Uiliq"、"Loulan"、"Niya Site"

Writers:Xiao Xiaoyong　Ruan Qiurong　Li Wenying

English Translation:Xiao Xiaoyong

Editor:Liu Yusheng

Photography:Liu Yusheng

封面字: 格土肯

封面: 塔克拉瑪干探險

神秘的塔里木

The Mystical Tarim

新疆對外文化交流協會

新 疆 人 民 出 版 社

前　言

從 1895—1935 年有許多外國學者、探險家到中國新疆塔里木盆地考察探險。這片在人類歷史發展和經濟文化交流中起過重要作用而后來幾乎被人們忘却了的土地，爲什么在 19 世紀末，20 世紀初又吸引了世人的注目呢？這里我們可以從最早的幾次對塔里木盆地的考察和探險中看得一清二楚。就以 1895 年到 1935 年曾先后多次到新疆的瑞典探險家斯文·赫定爲例，第一次在穿越塔克拉瑪干沙漠中，他雖然幾乎葬身沙海，但在他九死一生之后給塔克拉瑪干所下“死亡之海”的定義，即獲得了人們對他這次冒險生涯的敬慕，也使世人知道了世界上又一個可怖而神秘的地方——塔克拉瑪干。

四年之后，即 1899 年，在瑞典國王奧斯卡和百萬富翁諾貝爾的支持下，斯文·赫定再次進入塔克拉瑪干。這次他因爲發現了中國古代衛戍和貿易市鎮——樓蘭，并發掘了古代文書，考察了奇特的“雅丹”地貌而震驚了史學界和考古界。他的一系列發現引起了列强對中國西域文物的爭奪。1927—1935 年他本人又幾次到塔里木探險考察，前后相加，斯文·赫定在新疆的探險生活先后持續了四分之一世紀。

緊步斯氏后塵的就是出生于匈牙利的英國探險家斯坦因。他是以考古發掘和進行地理地貌測繪和人文考察的多種面目出現在塔里木盆地的。從 1900 年到 1914 年，他在絲綢之路古道的許多被沙漠淹没的中國漢(公元前至公元 1 世紀)、唐(公元 6 世紀)遺址中發掘和竊取大量古代文書、古錢幣、文物、寺廟壁畫而出了名。他也在廣大而特殊的地域進行了地理、民族、氣象、水文等方面的勘測和考察。

進行上述行徑的不僅是斯文·赫定和斯坦因，還有法國的伯希和，德國的範萊考克，俄國的尼古拉·普爾熱瓦爾斯基上校，日本的僧侶等等。他們也都曾在干旱難耐的戈壁沙漠追尋古人的踪迹，發掘過古墓、剥離過壁畫，描述過綠洲村落、河流湖泊的變遷。19 世紀末、20 世紀初，塔里木盆地確曾是考古和探險者的樂園。

這里我們把近代歷史中的這一幕幕驚心動魄的畫面作爲引子。那么 20 世紀的今天，再看這片大地。許多事物仍然會使人耳目一新。曾經聯結過世界的紐帶——絲綢之路，在 80 年代初期又被世人在絲路熱中重新認識。而在這片奇妙無比的大自然中又有些什么變异？這本畫册就是以西域故土的今天告訴人們，在人類進步、大自然的演進中，通過對新疆塔里木過去的回顧來認識它的今天和未來。尤其是通過塔克拉瑪干，人們稱之爲“死亡之海”的流動，沙漠的景觀，和近兩千年的變遷來印證當今世人所憂慮的一個問題——生態平衡。

因此，我們這本畫册以沙漠綠洲的變遷爲命題加以表現。而且以絲綢之路的興衰、變遷、沙漠遺址的發掘爲引綫。引深至塔里木沙漠生態、綠洲經濟、民族文化、開發建設等。我們認爲，塔克拉瑪干沙漠的流動變遷是有一定典型意義的。當然，新疆南部的沙漠不同于西亞、南亞乃至世界上的其他沙漠，因爲它是處于亞洲腹地，遠離海洋而被四面圍抱的山巒所隔絶封閉的全大陸性氣候。所以它既有同其它沙漠共有的特點，也有着自己特异的表現。一些外國科學家、旅游者來到塔里木，目睹了塔克拉瑪干沙漠之後，他們認爲這里是世界上最壯觀的沙漠。是的，從它腹部三四百英尺高的重叠的沙山和寸草不生的茫茫沙海到它四周邊沿和沙生植物群落，乃至圍攏它、劃破它的發源于四周昆侖山、帕米爾高原、喀喇昆侖山、天山、阿爾金山的條條河流所形成的綠色走廊、滋潤的片片綠洲構成了世界上一個特殊的地理環境。它展現出沙漠綠洲相互依存，相互排斥的生態關系；也包含着在這一生態環境中所形成的人們的一種特殊的精神風貌和歷史遺存。這些都會向人們展示出一幅幅奇妙的畫面，讓人們去探索歷史，探索自然和人的關系，水和綠洲在荒漠中的地位，從而給人類引伸出一個與大自然抗爭的新的未來。當然它也會以多種的民族習俗，光怪陸離的自然景觀、地理風貌，考古的新發現，自然的新變遷，以及人們建設改造的豐功偉績以饗讀者。

這一切的一切，就像塔里木在 19 世紀末，20 世紀初對于考古學家、地理學家和探險者同樣會有巨大的吸引力。

FOREWORD

Between the years of 1895 and 1935, many foreign scholars and adventurers came to explore and survey the Tarim Basin in Xinjiang, China. Why did this piece of land which had played such an important role in the development of human history and in economic and cultural exchange, and later almost completely forgotten, began to rekindle the attention of the world from the late19th century to the early 20th century? This can be answered by the several earliest investigations and explorations into the Tarim Basin. For example, take the activities of the Swedish explorer, Sven Hedin, who visited the Tarim Basin on several trips between theyears of 1895 and 1935. On his first trip he almost died in the desert, but after his miraculous escape he gave the Taklimakan Desert the name of "Sea of Death". His feats merited him awe and respect, and made known to the world the terrible and yet mystifying place – – the Taklmakan.

In 1899, four years after his initial trip, with the support of King Oscar of Sweden and the millionaire, Alfred Nobel, Sven Hedin returned to the Taklimakan. On this second trip he discovered the ancient Chinese garrison and trade town of Loulan, and unearthed ancient documents and investigated the unique 'Yardan' landforms which rocked historical and archaeological circles. His series of discoveries sparked the big powers' interests in rushing for the relics of the Western Territory of China. Sven Hedin himself came to the Tarim Basin several times between the years of 1927 and 1935 until China closed its doors. His exploration activities in Xinjiang continued, on and off, for a quarter of a century.

Following his footsteps was Aurel Stein, the Hungarian – British explorer, who engaged in archaeological diggings, geographical survey and cultural, anthropological research in the Tarim Basin. He is known for the amount of ancient documents, ancient coins, relics and murals he looted from the ruins of the Han Dynasty (B. C. to 1st century A. D.) and the Tang Dynasty (6th – century A. D.) along the ancient Silk Road which were buried in the desert. He also prospected and investigated the vast and unique territory from the fields of geography, ethnicity, meteorology, hydrology and others. Following in the footsteps of Sven Hedin and Aurel Stein were Bonin of France, von le Coq of Germany, Nicolai Przewalski of Russia, and various Japanese monks.

They, enduring the unbearable heat and drought of the gobi desert, had all come in search of the traces of ancient civilizations buried in the gobi desert. They excavated ancient tombs, peeled off murals, studied oasis villages and change in river courses. By the end of the 19th century and the early part of the 20th century, the Tarim Basin had become an archaeologists and explorers' Paradise. All that we have mentioned above, though shocking, is now history. Let us look at this vast piece of ancient land again in the 20th century, and we will discover many novelties. The Silk Road which once linked up the world, has been recognized anew in the '80s by a new interest in the Silk Road. What are the changes that have taken place on this vast area of the natural world? This journal is an attempt to answer that question. Through a retrospection of the past we can see the progress of mankind and the evolution of nature, and better understand the present and the future. Especially through the shifting sands of the desert we can confirm the changes the past two millenniums have brought and which worry mankind today, the question of ecological balance.

Therefore, we have chosen as the theme of this journal the change in the desert oases, and using the rise and decline of the Silk Road, its changes and the excavations of its desert ruins as a lead to subjects such as the Tarim desert ecology, oasis economy, ethnic culture, development and construction, and others. We believe that there is typical meaning in the shift and change of the Taklimakan Desert. Naturally, the deserts in South Xinjiang are different from those found in West Asia, South Asia, or even other places of the world because the deserts here are in the hinterland of Asia, remote from any ocean, surrounded and sealed off by towering mountains, having its complete continental climate. Therefore they have common characteristics with other deserts of the world and yet they also have their unique characteristics. Scientists and tourists from overseas who have visited the Tarim Basin and seen the Taklimakan Desert for themselves all say that it is the most spectacular desert in the world. They are right. Its unique geographical surroundings range from the 300 – 400 foot high overlapping sand hills to barren stretches of sand, to clusters of sand vegetation along its edges, even to the many streams and rivers which flow from the Pamir Plateau, the Kunlun and Karakoram Mountains, Tianshan Mountains, and Altun Mountains which cut off the desert to form a green corridor, nurturing scattered oases that make up this unique geographical environment in the world. The desert and the oases are mutually dependent and yet the relationship between their ecology is mutually repelling, including the unique spirit of the people and the historical remains of the land that is formed by that ecological environment. These changes, reflected in wonderful pictures, help us to explore history, and the relationship between nature and man, and the importance of water in the oases of the desert, hence pointing out a way to combat nature in the future. The journal also acquaints the reader with the colorful customs of the multi – ethnic peoples, strange, natural landscapes, geograhical features, new discoveries in archaeology, new changes in nature, and man's achievements in developing and transforming the land.

All these have as much, if not more, attraction for the readers than they did for the archealogists, geographers, and explorers ofthe Tarim at the end of the 19th century and the early 20th century.

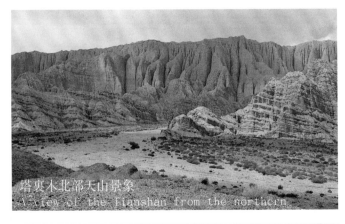
塔裏木北部天山景象
A view of the Tianshan from the northern

塔裏木西緣昆侖景象
A view of the Kunlun Mountains from the southern side of the Tarim.

慕士塔格冰峰
Ice-capped peaks of the Muztag.

阿爾金山之景
A view of the Altun Mountains.

Tourist Map of the Silk Road in Xinjiang

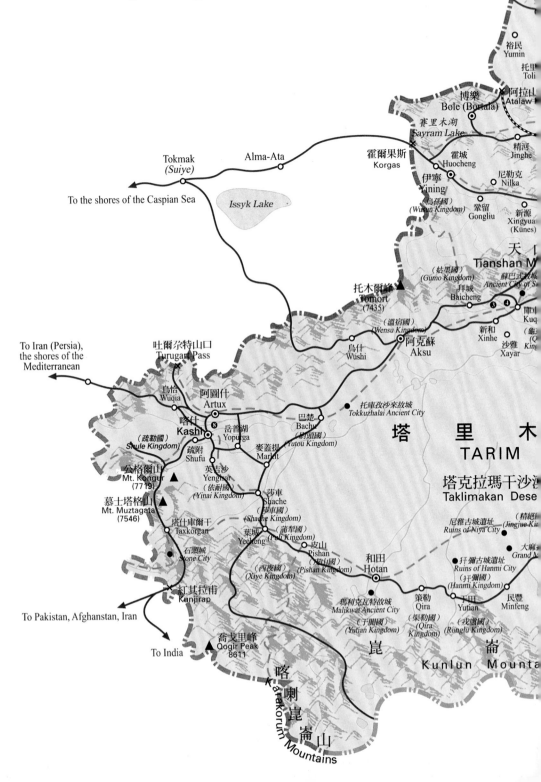

裕民 Yumin
托里 Toli
阿拉山 Atalaw
博樂 Bole (Borlala)
賽里木湖 Sayram Lake
霍爾果斯 Korgas
霍城 Huocheng
精河 Jinghe
尼勒克 Nilka
伊寧 Yining
(烏孫國) (Wusun Kingdom)
鞏留 Gongliu
新源 (庫) Xingyua (Künes)
天 Tianshan M
(姑墨國) (Gumo Kingdom)
蘇巴什故城 Ancient City of S
拜城 Baicheng
庫車 Kuq
新和 Xinhe
沙雅 Xayar
Tokmak (Suiye)
Alma-Ata
To the shores of the Caspian Sea
Issyk Lake
托木爾峰 Tomort (7435)
(溫宿國) (Wensu Kingdom)
烏什 Wushi
阿克蘇 Aksu
To Iran (Persia), the shores of the Mediterranean
吐爾尕特山口 Turugart Pass
阿圖什 Artux
烏恰 Wuqia
托庫孜沙來故城 Tokkuzhalai Ancient City
巴楚 Bachu
(尉頭國) (Yutou Kingdom)
喀什 Kashi
岳普湖 Yopurga
塔 里 木 TARIM
(疏勒國) Shule Kingdom
疏附 Shufu
麥蓋提 Markit
塔克拉瑪干沙漠 Taklimakan Dese
公格爾山 Mt. Kongur (7719)
英吉沙 Yengisar
(依耐國) (Yinai Kingdom)
莎車 Shache
(莎車國) (Shache Kingdom)
慕士塔格山 Mt. Muztagata (7546)
尼雅古城遺址 Ruins of Niya City
(精絕國) (Jingjue Kingdom)
塔什庫爾干 Taxkorgan
葉城 Yecheng
(蒲犁國) (Puli Kingdom)
皮山 Pishan
(西夜國) (Xiye Kingdom)
(皮山國) (Pishan Kingdom)
和田 Hotan
扞彌古城遺址 Ruins of Hanmi City
(扞彌國) (Hanmi Kingdom)
大麻 Grand N
石頭城 Stone City
紅其拉甫 Kunjirap
瑪利克瓦特故城 Malikwat Ancient City
(于闐國) (Yutian Kingdom)
策勒 Qira
(集勒國) (Qira Kingdom)
于田 Yutian
(戎盧國) (Ronglu Kingdom)
民豐 Minfeng
To Pakistan, Afghanistan, Iran
To India
喬戈里峰 Qogir Peak 8611
崑 崙 Kunlun Mountain
喀喇崑崙山 Karakorum Mountains

新疆
XINJIANG

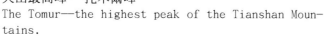

天山最高峰—托木爾峰
The Tomur—the highest peak of the Tianshan Mountains.

塔克拉瑪干南緣的和田綠洲
Oases on the southern edge of the Taklimakan Desert.

塔里木盆地的日出
Sunrise in the Tarim Basin.

塔克拉瑪干沙漠中的季節河──和田河
The Hotan River —— a seasonal river in the Taklimakan
Desert.　　(By Wu Bing)

塔里木河下游的維吾爾族村落（武　斌　攝）
A Uygur village at the lower reaches of the Tarim River.

塔里木北部的戈壁绿洲
Oasis in the gobi at north of the Tarim Basin.

無疆的野馬
——塔里木河

　　塔里木河位于塔里木盆地北部,流向由西到東,是中國最長的內陸河。從支流葉爾羌河上源算起,全長 2127 公里,流域面積 19.8 萬平方公里。塔里木河的支流有玉龍喀什河、喀喇喀什河匯流而成的和田河以及葉爾羌、阿克蘇河;在上個世紀還有喀什噶爾河。近年來,葉爾羌河由于上游攔水灌溉等原因,除洪水期外已基本上斷絕了與塔里木河的聯系。和田河僅在年洪水期有余水進入塔里木河。只有阿克蘇河長流不斷,供給了塔里木河全部水量的四分之三。

　　千百年來,人們向往它、探索它、謳歌它,有關它的記載、傳文不絕于書。

　　最早記載當推公元前的《山海經》"河出昆侖,潛行地下,至蔥嶺山于闐國,復分岐流出,合而東注泑澤,至而復行積石,爲中國河"。塔里木河現在的這一名稱見于《清史稿》,它是維吾爾語,意爲"無疆之馬",這條河經常改變河道,橫冲直闖,真像一匹無疆的野馬。塔里木河出自巍巍天山,莽莽昆侖,逶迤蜿蜒于塔克拉瑪干大沙漠的西北和東部,形成曾溝通了中國內地與西方的一條天然陸路通道,是古代"絲綢之路"的必經之路。因此,沿河一帶留下了不少古代文明的遺址,也滋潤了沿岸幾個盛産糧棉、瓜果的經濟作物區。

　　塔里木河,是一條在歷史上赫赫有名的河流,也是流經沙漠、戈壁的一條奇妙的河。

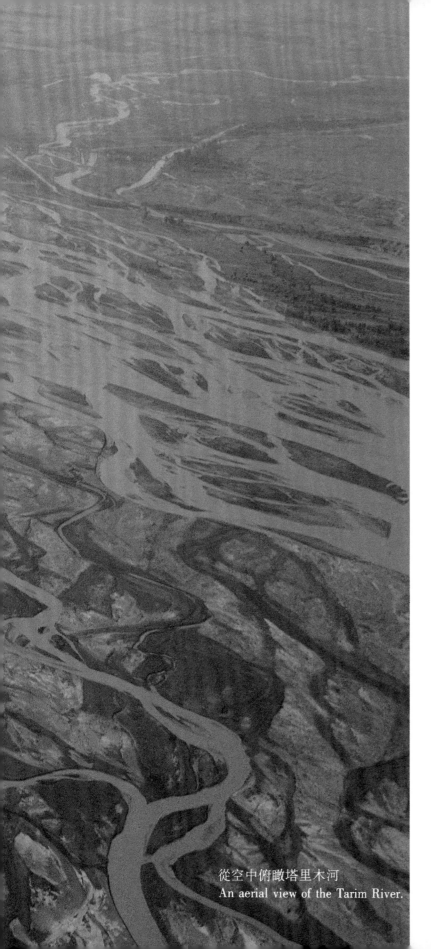

從空中俯瞰塔里木河
An aerial view of the Tarim River.

THE REINLESS WILD HORSE
—— THE TARIM RIVER

The Tarim River is located at the north of the Tarim Basin, flowing from west to east, and is China's longest inland river. Measuring from its tributary source at the Yerqiang River, it is 2, 127 kilometers long and covers an area of 198, 000 square kilometers. Tributaries of the Tarim River include the Hotan River, the Yerqiang River, and the Aksu River which are fed by the converged Ulungur Kash and the Karakash Rivers, in the last century it also included the Kashgar River. But in recent years, due to the construction of irrigation dams at the upper reaches of the Yerqiang River, these rivers are no longer connected to the Tarim River except in flood seasons. It is only when the Hotan River is in flood that surplus water runs into the Tarim River. The Aksu River is the only river that flows all year, its excess flow makes up for three – fourths the volume that of the Tarim River.

For the last millennium or more, the Tarim River has repeatedly appeared in historical records as an object of study and praise.

It was initially recorded in Shanhaijin, a work which appeared over two thousand years ago, which described it as ' originating from the Kunlun Mountains, flowing into the earth, and remerging on the plateau of the state of Yutien, then flowing out in various tributaries, then converging and flows east into Youze, to Jishi, to become China River ' . The name "Tarim" first appeared in a Qing Dynasty record, which in Uygur meant ' an unreined horse ' because it changed courses frequently and "galloped" about madly like a reinless horse. The Tarim River originates from the lofty Tianshan and Kunlun Mountains, and winds its way to the northwestern and eastern part of the great Taklimakan Desert, forming a natural land passage connecting the interior of China with the West, once the thoroughfare of the ancient Silk Road. Therefore, it not only accounted for the various ruins of ancient civilizations found along its shores, but it also nurtured the land which produced grain and cotton in abundance, not to mention fruit and melon and other cash crops.

The Tarim River is also a historically well – known river, a magical river which flows through the desert and the gobi.

塔里木河下游的胡杨林及沙生植物生态
An ecological environment of the diversi – form leaved poplar and desert vegetation at the lower reaches of the Tarim River.

鳥瞰塔克拉瑪干大沙漠的茫茫沙海
A bird's – eye view of the vast Taklimakan Desert.

沙漠 · 戈壁 · 緑野

塔里木盆地地處亞洲腹部，是地球上離海洋最遠的地方，它的周圍，幾乎全是巍峨的群山，廣大的高原。這些山地平均海拔高度都在4000 至 5000 米以上。塔里木盆地深藏在大陸腹心的地理位置，構成了它特殊的地理地貌和生態環境。

塔里木盆地氣候極端干燥，降水稀少，蒸發大大超過降水量，氣溫的年較差和日較差也都極大。尤其是在夏季，輻射强盛，溫差懸殊，使盆地邊緣年平均降雨量只有 30—50 毫米，盆地腹部的沙漠地帶少于 20 毫米甚至 5 毫米，而且蒸發量却在 2500—3400 毫米。由于干旱和炎熱便形成了荒漠和半荒漠的地理景觀。但在同一個干燥的環境下，因地形和人文情况的不同，它大體上可以分爲幾個層次和幾種景觀帶：最内爲鹽湖帶，分布有大面積的鹽碱土，僅生長些極耐鹽碱的稀疏草類和灌木，成爲鹽湖景觀；外爲沙漠帶，植物極少，成爲沙丘起伏的荒漠景觀；再外爲沃野帶，植被主要爲耐干旱耐鹽碱的灌木和喬木，土壤灌溉后多成爲灰鈣土，有利于灌溉農業的發展，成爲沃野景觀；再外爲山麓礫石帶，礫石暴露，草木稀少，水多潛伏地下，成爲荒涼的戈壁景觀。總的説來，塔里木盆地境内植被極爲稀疏，主要生長旱生灌木和耐旱草類，代表土壤爲含有不同鹽度的漠鈣土類，且多爲未發育土壤。

塔里木盆地礫石戈壁的形成主要是高山雪水冲刷了風化的山岩碎屑，把夾帶的砂礫搬運到山麓地方，因水流速度驟減積成。

塔里木盆地中沃野的面積大小不一，它們都是以 10—2500 平方公里不等的綠洲出現在整個盆地。沃野總面積爲 14600 平方公里，約占盆地面積的六十分之一。它與山的高度和雪源的多寡有極密切的關系。像疏勒沃野面積爲 2650 平方公里，莎車沃野面積爲 2600 平方公里，而在山勢較低的東部盆地，氣候干燥，水源不足，因此沃野分布也較少。像若羌沃野面積僅 30 平方公里。

從沃野帶向内，不是沙丘累累，便是戈壁暴露，成爲一片廣大而荒涼的地方，這就是沙漠帶，也是世界第二大流動性沙漠，33 萬多平方公里的塔克拉瑪干。

塔里木沙漠的形成是由地岩石受機械風化崩裂成碎屑和細沙形成的。盆地内的湖水干涸后的湖底砂泥也是流沙的一個主要來源。這一片沙海，形成許多平均高達 90 米左右的新月形沙丘、沙崗和沙脊。它們的分布很規律，大部分與從庫魯克山吹來的干熱風以及來自干燥的蒙古、西伯利亞反氣旋的分支，由東北部向塔里木盆地方向侵入有關。因此，這里所有荒漠上的新月型沙丘、沙崗和沙脊，它們的緩坡一律面向北偏東，陡坡一律面向西偏南。沙丘、沙崗和沙脊此起彼伏，正像大海波浪一樣。

在沙漠中心，没有植物，也没有野獸，甚至連飛鳥蟲類都很少，完全是一片荒涼寂静的地方。

塔里木盆地的中部東端爲著名的羅布泊，那里地勢較低，塔里木河水匯集成爲鹽湖，因此，這一帶又稱鹽湖帶。但是由于羅布泊的游移，現在這里的湖泊已干涸多年。只有那無邊無際的"土丘林"，令人神秘莫測，那就是著名的"雅丹"地貌。它是干燥地區的一種特殊地貌，由一系列平行的"壟脊"和"溝槽"構成，順盛行風方向伸展。雅丹地形以羅布泊北面最典型，分布也最廣泛。這在世界上也屬罕見。

羅布泊盆地，歷史上有鹽湖和沼澤密布。據現在的沙漠考察人員講，羅布泊盆底有大量的鹽類品，成爲塔里木盆地現代積鹽中心。

羅布泊的往返遷移，留下的古河床，是一個無人區，這里的地表凝結成一片鹽殼，在長期東北風的影響下形成一種爲東北風相垂直的坡狀地形。所以在這里旅行十分艱難。

DESERT. GOBI. VERDANT PLAINS.

The Tarim Basin is located in the hinterland of Asia, furthest removed from any outlet to the sea, almost completely surrounded by lofty mountains and vast plateaus. The average elevation of the mountains range above 4, 000 – 5, 000 meters sea level. Its geographical location accounts for its u-nique landform and ecological environment.

The climate of the Tarim Basin is extremely arid with little precipita-tion, and often its evaporation exceeds its precipitation volume, with huge differences in its year – round and daily temperatures. Especially in the summer when there is strong radiation and huge differences in daily tem-perature. Its annual precipitation is only around 30 – 50 millemeters and less than 20 millimeters, or as little as 5 millimeters in the desert at the interior of the Basin, but its evaporation is at 2500 – 3400 millemeters. Its barren and semi – barren geographical features are the result of the drought and heat. However, the environment can be divided into several 'circles' and landscape belts according to the difference in terrain and human culture. The innermost circle is the salt lakelandscape where the vast area is saline – al-kali soil on which only grass and shrubbery which are extremely resistant to salt and alkali are very sparsely grown, commonly known as the salt lake landscape belt; the circle outside it is covered with undulating sandhills, making it the desert landscape belt; the outer circle is the fertile plain where the vegetation is extremely drought and saline – alkali resistant shrubbery and trees, and the soil turns to dust or becomes calcified after irrigation which is conducive to the development of irrigated agriculture, making it the fertile plain landscape belt; the outermost ring is the mountain slope gravel circle where the ground is exposed and vegetation is sparse, and most of the water runs underground, making it the gobi landscape belt. In general, vegetation is sparse in the Tarim Basin, and whatever there is are mostly dry land shrubbery and drought resistant species of grass, and the typical soil is calcified with different degrees of salinity, and most of it is immature soil.

The gobi in the Tarim is formed by the snowmelt from towering moun-tains that carry the weathered rock down to the slopes and accumulated there by the ebbing flow.

The fertile plains in the Tarim Basin vary in range and they usually appear as oases measuring 10 – 2, 500 square kilometers. The entire area of the fertile plains is 14, 600 square kilometers, making up for one – sixtieth the total area of the Basin. The number and size of the oases are closely related to the altitude and quantity in precipitation of the nearby moun-tains. For instance, the Shule fertile plains measure 2, 650 square kilome-ters, and the Shache fertile plains measure 2, 600 square kilometers, whereas the east of the Basin where the mountains are of much lower altitude and the climate is more arid and there is a lack of water, the distribution of

fertile plain as an example, it only measures about 30 square kilometers.

Going inward from the fertile plains one sees little else but countless sand hills or endless stretches of gobi, barren and wasted, and that is the desert belt, also known as the world's second largest shifting desert, cover-ing an area of over 330, 000 square kilometers —— the Taklimakan.

The Tarim desert is formed by weathered fragments of rocks and fine sand. The main source of the shifting sand is from the lake bottoms of dried up lake beds of the Basin. This sea of sand formed many crescent – shaped sand hills, sand dunes and ridges reaching a height of around 90 me-ters. They are regularly distributed in the Tarim Basin according to the influx of the dry heat from the Kuruktag, from Mongolia, and the branches of re-verse air currents from Siberia which blow from the northeast of the Basin which account for the gradual sloping of the sand hills, sand dunes, and ridges all facing the north – northeasterly direction, and their steeper slopes all facing the west – southwesterly direction. The undulating sand hills, dunes, and ridges of the desert resemble waves in the ocean.

The heart of the desert is devoid of plants and beasts, and even birds and insects are rarely seen, and the land is a completely barren and wasted.

At the eastern edge of the center of the Tarim Basin is the famous Lopnur, which is at a relatively low elevation, is a salt lake resulting from the convergence of waters from the Tarim River. So it is known as the salt lake belt. However, due to the constant change in course of the Lopnur, this lake has been dried for many years. The endless stretches of hills, which appear so mystical, is known as the 'Yardan' landform, which is a unique landform found in arid regions, made up of a series of parallel ridges and troughs which run in the direction of the wind. The most typical 'Yardan' landforms are found north of the Lopnur, and their distribution is vast. A phenomena rarely found elsewhere in the world.

Historically, the Lopnur Basin had densely distributed salt lakes and marshy swamps. According to present – day desert surveyors, there are great quantities of multiple varieties of salts at the bottom of the Lopnur Basin, and it has become the center of salt accumulation of the Tarim Basin.

The constant change of the Lopnur has left behind an ancient riverbed which is a no – man's land, covered by a crust of crystallized salt, and due to the permanent northeasterly winds, the land is a series of slope – like forms vertical to the northeasterly winds, hence traveling in the area is es-pecially difficult.

博斯騰湖開滿荷花,勝似江南
Blooming lotus on Lake Bosteng, a picture of 'south of the Yangtse.'

流沙不斷侵入的博斯騰湖
Shifting sand assaulting Lake Bosteng.

沙漠不斷淹没的胡楊林
A forest of diversi – form leaved poplar being engulfed by the desert.

沙漠深處的柯里亞河灣小綠洲
A small oasis at the bay of the Keriya River deep in the desert.

原始胡杨林中的大胡杨树
A giant in a primitive diversi-form leaved poplar forest

生長在沙丘上的胡楊林
A forest of diversi – form leaved poplar on sandhills.

手持獵隼的維吾爾人
A Uygur hunter with a falcon.

于田縣荒漠中的人家
A family in the desert of Yutien County.

位于塔里木西部绿洲最大的历史文化名城——喀什噶尔
Kashgar —— the biggest historical and cultural city located in the oasis west of the Tarim Basin.

塔里木已成爲中國著名棉花生産地區
The Tarim Basin —— China's well – known
cotton production base.

和田綠洲千里葡萄長廊（武 斌 攝）
The thousand – mile Grape Corridor of the
Hotan Oasis.　　　(By Wu Bing)

塔里木河畔生産建設兵團農場水稻豐收
Rice harvest on a Production and Construction
Corps farm along the shores of the Tarim River.

世界第二大沙漠——塔克拉瑪干沙漠

被稱之爲"死亡之海"的塔克拉瑪干沙漠，位于 56 萬平方公里的塔里木盆地的腹部。整個沙漠東西長約 1000 余公里，南北寬約 400 多公里，總面積 337600 平方公里。塔克拉瑪干占全國沙漠面積的 47.3%，是中國最大的沙漠，也是世界上的七大沙漠之一。

塔克拉瑪干沙漠，系暖溫帶干旱沙漠，酷暑最高溫度達 67.2℃，晝夜溫差達 40℃ 以上；平均年降水不超過 100 毫米，最底只有四五毫米；而平均蒸發量高達 2500—3400 毫米。全年有三分之一是風沙日，大風風速每秒達 300 米。由于整個沙漠受西北和南北兩個盛行風向的交叉影響，風沙活動十分頻繁而劇烈，流動沙丘占 80% 以上。據測算底矮的沙丘每年可移動約 20 米，近一千年來，整個沙漠向南伸延了約 100 公里。絲路古道南道的精絕、小宛、戎盧、圩彌、渠樂、樓蘭等古代城鎮和許多村落都被流沙所湮没。

由于地處歐亞大陸的中心，四面爲高山環繞，塔克拉瑪干沙漠充滿了奇幻和神秘的色彩。變幻多樣的沙漠形態，豐富而抗鹽碱風沙的沙生植物植被，蒸發量高于降水量的干旱氣候，以及尚存于沙漠中的湖泊，穿越沙海的綠洲，潛入沙漠的河流，生存于沙漠中的野生動物和飛禽昆蟲等；特别是被深埋于沙海中的絲路遺址、遠古村落、地下石油及多種金屬礦藏都被籠罩在神奇的迷霧之中，有待于人們去探尋。

THE WORLD'S SECOND LARGEST DESERT
—— THE TAKLIMAKAN

Known as the 'sea of death', the Taklimakan Desert is located in the hinter part of the Tarim Basin which is 560, 000 kilometers in area. The desert stretching from east to west measures over 1, 000 kilometers, and from north to south over 400 kilometers, covering an area of 337, 600 square kilometers. The Taklimakan Desert makes up for 47.3% of the total desert area of China, and it is the country 's biggest desert, and considered one of the seven big deserts in the world.

The Taklimakan is an arid desert in the temperate belt. Its highest temperature is recorded at 67.2 degrees Celsius, with a difference of above 40 degrees Celsius within the 24 – hour day; average precipitation less than 100 millemeters, and as little as 4 – 5 millemeters; but its average evaporation is as high as 2, 500 – 3, 400 millemeters. Sandstorms blow four months out of the year, and the wind velocity reaches 300 meters per second. Because the entire desert is influenced by the cross – blowing of winds from the north and the south, its sandstorms are extremely frequent and fierce, and shifting sandhills make up over 80% of the desert. In a survey of sand hills of lesser heights, each year they shift for about 20 meters, so within the last millennium, the entire desert has shifted southward for about 100 kilometers. Ancient states and cities along the Silk Road, such as Jinjue, Xiaowan, Ronglu, Yumi, Qule and Loulan, and countless villages have been buried by the shiftiing sand.

Because the Taklimakan is located in the center of the Eurasian continent and surrounded by towering peaks, it is full of fantasy and mysticism. The ever – changing form of the desert, its highly salt and wind resistant desert plants and vegetation, its evaporation – exceeding – precipitation arid climate, its lakes in the desert, its oases, its rivers that run under the desert, and its wild animals, birds, and insects, especially its Silk Road ruins which are now buried by the sand, its ancient villages, its deposits of oil and rich varieties of natural resources are all shrouded in mystery, awaiting man's discovery and exploration.

塔克拉瑪干大沙漠 The Great Taklimakan Desert.

塔克拉瑪干沙漠景觀　A view of the Taklimakan Desert.

沙漠腹地一瞥 A view of the desert interior.

起伏無窮的沙壠 Limitless undulating sand dunes.

羅布泊雅丹地貌
The 'Yardan' landform in the Lopnur.

沙漠中干涸的胡楊　Withered diversi – form leaved poplar in the desert.

羅布泊中的雅丹地貌　The 'Yardan' landform in the Lopnur.

沙漠中干涸的胡楊　Withered diversi – form leaved poplar in the desert.

沙丘頂端的紅柳
The red – willow on top of sand dunes.

奇妙的沙紋
Wondrous 'designs' on the sand.

新月形沙丘 Crescent – shaped sand dunes.

沙漠冬季景觀
Winter scene in the desert.

沙生植物植被 Desert vegetation.

塔克拉玛干腹部沙漠河干涸后的景象
A view of a dried-up river in the desert interior.

沙漠居民引洪之后沙丘之間出現的植被
Vegetation appears after residents flooded the desert.

安迪爾沙漠河 A desert river in Andier County

民豐縣沙漠中的魚湖
A fishing lake in the desert of Minfeng County

在塔克拉瑪干沙漠中野駱駝的保護區
A nature reserve for wild camels in the Taklimakan Desert.

同戈壁形同一體的蜥蜴 A lizard blending into the gobi.

戈壁灘上所見到的海市蜃樓 Mirage found on the gobi.

沙漠東部戈壁灘的風化石
Weathered rock on the gobi east of the desert.

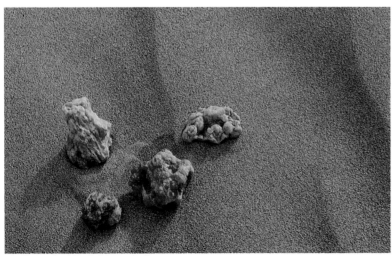

沙漠上看到的奇妙的瑪瑙石 Marvelous agate seen in the desert.

頑强與沙漠抗争的沙生植物
Desert plants braving the assault of the sand.

于田縣綠洲邊的金字塔沙山　A sand 'pyramid' at the edge of an oasis in Yutien County.

沙海中叢生的紅柳與胡楊
Clusters of red will and diversi – form leaved poplar in the desert.

塔克拉瑪干腹地打出的新水源　New source of water found in the Taklimakan Desert interior.

生長在新月形沙丘上胡楊
Diversi – form leaved poplar growing on the crescent – shaped sand hills.

鳥瞰塔里木北部絲路古道的烽遂　A bird's-eye view of a smoke signal tower on the ancient Silk Road.

古 道 烽 燧

　　塔里木盆地的烽燧驛站,歷史悠長。建于秦漢的長城自敦煌西出玉門關之后,便以烽燧墩臺的形式出現在西去的古道上。座座烽燧自樓蘭環繞塔里木到帕米爾高原; 從哈密沿天山北麓到伊犁河谷都可以看到它們的身影 。在被戈壁和流沙所隔絕的綠洲之間烽燧驛站的設置保護了絲路古道的暢通。因此,沿着點點烽燧的走向,在相隔一定的距離,既有屯兵的關所 ,又有專供來往客商、僧侶和使者留宿打尖的驛站。今天,當你來到戈壁灘頭和沙漠邊緣, 那高聳的墩臺和關所驛站的遺迹仍然像路標一樣屹立在那里,會焕起當今旅人思古之幽情。

SMOKE SIGNAL TOWERS ON THE ANCIENT SILK ROAD

The smoke signal relay stations in the Tarim Basin has had a very long history. They appeared after the Jin-Han Dynasty built the Great Wall which reached Dunhuang and stretched further west to the Yumen Pass. These smoke signal relay stations were built all the way from where the Great Wall ended to encircle Loulan and eventually reached from the Tarim Basin to the Pamir Plateau; and they can be seen from Hami, along the northern slope of the Tianshan Mountains all the way to the Ili River valley. These smoke signal towers or relay stations serve to protect the oases isolated by the gobi or the shifting sand, and to ensure the flow of traffic on the ancient Silk Road. Therefore, following the direction of the smoke signal relay stations at regular intervals there are garrison soldiers and stations that provide board and lodging for traveling merchants, monks, or envoys. Today, when one comes to the gobi and the edge of the desert and see the smoke signal towers still standing erect like road markers, one cannot help but be overwhelmed by nostalgia.

在烽火臺旁邊見到的旋風　Whirl wind seen beside a smoke signal tower.

在戈壁蒼茫中屹立的古代烽遂驛站
An ancient way station still standing on the barren gobi.

建于漢代著名的克孜尕哈烽火臺
The famous ancient smoke signal tower of Kizgahar, built during the Han Dynasty.

被湮没的文明

塔里木盆地的南端是古丝綢之路的重要路段。由于受到流沙的不斷侵擾，近兩千年來已有三百多個村鎮和古城被向南移動的塔克拉瑪干沙漠吞噬湮没，成爲埋没着許多古代文化遺産的地區，吸引着國内外考古工作者、探險家、旅游者。塔克拉瑪干沙漠的名稱，包含着維吾爾語中"湮埋在沙漠底下的住所"和"財寶被埋没的地方"的寓意，這里的地下寶藏早就被當地的居民所發現。1870年有兩個當地人到和田周圍那些被埋没的古城中挖掘珍寶，其中一個就帶回了兩尊佛像，另一個人則帶回了幾個金指環、鼻環和一些硬幣。當時它們都落入了歐洲人之手，這也是塔克拉瑪干丢失的第一批文物。正是這一信息，從19世紀末到

20世紀初，一些外國探險家接踵而至，他們從沙漠廢墟中，發現并挖掘了許多比金錢更加珍貴的佉盧文、梵文、吐火羅文、漢文等文字的木簡、木牘、木函、文書以及古錢幣、壁畫、塑像、木板畫和絲綢、陶俑等等。這一地下埋藏也可從近代尼雅遺址的不斷出土乃至樓蘭、若羌縣米蘭的考察發掘中得到證實。就目前而言，隨着流沙的移動而露出地表，和已被考古工作者發現的，僅塔克拉瑪干沙漠東南緣和田至且末、若羌一綫就有約特干、馬力克瓦特、山普拉古墓葬、丹丹烏力克、卡孜那克佛寺遺址，以及位于民豐縣安迪爾沙漠河末端的阿克斯皮爾（公元6世紀所建蘭城鎮）和且末縣古墓葬、若羌瓦古峽遺址等等。

BURIED CIVILIZATIONS

The southern end of the Tarim Basin had been a very important section of the ancient Silk Road. Under the constant assault of the shifting sands, over three hundred villages, towns, and cities have been buried by the southward shifting Taklimakan in the last thousand years, making it a region where there are many ruins and relics of ancient civilizations, drawing archaeologists, explorers, and tourists from all around the world. The Takli-makan, in Uygur, has an implied meaning of "homes buried under the sand" and "where riches are buried" because its underground treasures had been discovered by local residents early on. In 1870, two local residents went to the vicinity of Hotan to dig for treasures in the buried ancient cities and one of them came back with two Buddha statues, while the other brought back several gold rings, nose rings and some coins. These finds later found their way into European hands, and were the first batch of relics taken from the Taklimakan. This started the stream of foreign adventurers who came between the end of the 19th century and the early 20th century to excavate the desert ruins, and discovered many relics more valuable than gold, such as wooden tablets, wooden letters, wooden letters and documents written in Tocharian, Sanskrit, Tuhuolu and Chinese, and ancient coins, murals, statues, drawings on wood, silks and clay figurines. These underground riches can be further proved by the modern excavations done, and finds discovered in the ruins of Niya, Loulan, and Milan in Rouqiang County. Presently, archaeologists have worked on the grounds exposed by the shifting desert, and merely in the area of the southeastern rim of the Taklimakan Desert alone from Hotan to Qiemo, were discovered burial sites of Yurtkan, Malikwat, and Shanpula, and Buddhist temple ruins in Dandanulik, Kiznak, and at the end of the desert river in Andier in Minfeng County, ancient Akspier (the township of Lancheng built in 6th century A.D.) plus ancient burial sites in Qiemo County and the ancient ruins of Wagu Gorge of Rouqiang.

考古工作者來到沙漠古城
Archaeologists visiting a ruin in the desert.

位于塔克拉玛干沙漠南缘被沙漠淹埋的建于公元 6 世纪的兰城镇遗址
Buried ruins of Lancheng township(6th century A. D.), southern edge of the Taklimakan Desert.

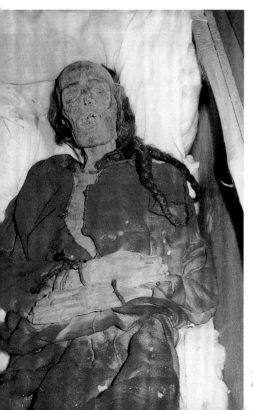

公元 1 世纪,山普拉墓葬中出土的缕空织物
Ist Century A. D. open – work fabric unearthed in the Shanpula tombs.

且末县墓葬中出土的脸部绘有花纹的约 3000 年的干尸
Approximately 3000 – year old dried corpse with tatooed face unearthed in Qiemo County.

在和田沙漠中保護古城的老人
An elderly caretaker of an ancient ruin in the desert of Hotan.

塔克拉瑪干南部沙漠深處公元6世紀的阿克斯皮爾古城遺址,半閉半開的城
至今還很完好
A well－preserved, half－open city gate of the Akspier ruins of 6th Century A.
in the heart of the southern part of the Taklimakan.

從空中看到被茫茫沙海吞没的村落
An aerial view of a village swallowed by the desert.

絲 路 遺 迹

新疆是中國開辟絲綢之路的重要地段。早在公元前一百多年到公元 10 世紀左右海上絲綢之路開通之前，它曾是連接歐亞大陸的一條重要陸路通道，爲東西方經濟、文化的交往作出了不可磨滅的歷史貢獻。而塔里木盆地，則是從中國的漢、唐時期開辟的絲綢之路的最早的路段。它環繞塔里木盆地，曾經經歷過异常繁忙的時期。從最早的絲綢、瓷器、造紙、鑄鐵術等的西去，到藥材、瓜果、珠寶和佛教的東傳進行了頻繁的交往。可以説在這條大道上，當時商賈、使者、僧侶川流不息。中國唐代（公元 7 世紀）高僧玄奘西去印度取經之后，所著《大唐西域記》中描述過它的地理風光、民族風情、歷史傳説；而著名的意大利旅行家馬可·波羅也曾記録過翻越帕米爾高原的艱辛，喀什噶爾的繁榮，以及沿途的見聞，個人的經歷。今天在塔里木盆地南北兩條古道上，甚至在塔克拉瑪干沙漠深處，依然留存着反映古絲綢之路經濟、文化的許多遺迹。

塔里木盆地的絲路遺址，千余年來，雖然經歷了漫長的歷史，而一度被人們忘却。但是到了 19 世紀末 20 世紀初，它又成了人們研究考察、探險踏訪的熱點。當時來自瑞典、英國、德國、法國、俄國、日本等衆多的探險家，曾在塔里木盆地的四周和塔克拉瑪干沙漠深處，有過許多重要的發現，并對壁畫、佛像、各類古代文書和其他文物進行了大量的剥離和發掘。到了本世紀，隨着中國學者的發現和研究，70 年代末期又興起了一次研究和探索絲綢之路古道的熱潮。特别是在對絲綢之路沿綫宗教文化、音樂美術、經濟地理、民族變遷的研究中形成了以敦煌、吐魯番、庫車、克孜爾石窟藝術、樓蘭興亡爲研究中心的絲綢之路學。1989 年聯合國還專門組織專家學者對絲路沿途進行了考察。

TRACES OF ANCIENT CIVILIZATIONS ALONG THE SILK ROAD

Xinjiang is an important location in the opening up of the ancient Silk Road. Before the opening up of the sea route of the ancient Silk Road between the last century B. C. and 10th century A. D., it had been an important land passagè which connected the continents of Europe and Asia, and its historical contribution toward East – West economic and cultural interchanges cannot be obliterated. The Tarim Basin, one of the very earliest sections of the ancient Silk Road had been opened from the Han – Tang Dynasty times. The road circled the Tarim Basin, and had been a very busy thoroughfare with the earliest interchanges marked by the westward flow of silk, china, paper – making, iron – casting techniques and the eastward dissemination of medicinal herbs, fruit and melon, gems and jewelry and Buddhist sutras. We can safely say that on this stretch of the Silk Road there had been an endless flow of merchants, envoys and monks. After the Tang Dynasty monk, Xuanzang, went to India in quest of the Buddhist Sutra in the 6th century, wrote "Records of theWestern Territory of the Tang Dynasty" which described all the geographical features, the ethnic customs, and historical legends of the places which he had passed through, and the famous Italian traveller, Marco Polo also had recorded hardships encountered in crossing the Pamir Plateau, prosperity in Kashgar, and all that he had seen and experienced on his journey. Today, there are still many historical ruins on the northern and southern passages of the ancient Silk Road, and even deep in the heart of the Taklimakan Desert that reflect the past economy and culture of ancient towns on that road.

The Silk Road ruins in the Tarim Basin have a long – standing history, and had, at one time, been forgotten. However, between the late 19th century and the early 20th century, it reemerged as a focal point of interest for investigation and exploration. Explorers from Sweden Britain, Germany, France, Russia, Japan and other countries came to the surrounding areas of the Tarim Basin and the heart of the Taklimakan Desert and made many discoveries. They peeled off murals, excavated buddhist statues, various ancient documents and other relics. With the discovery and research of Chinese scholars in the present century, another wave of interest in the ancient Silk Road was aroused in the '70s, especially on the religion, culture, music, art, economic geography, and ethnic customs which formed a new Silk Road study focusing on the cave art of Dunhuang, Turpan, Kuqa, and Kizil, and also the rise and fall of Loulan. In 1989, the United Nations had organized a team of experts to survey along the Silk Road.

位于喀什古城近郊的約建于公元 6 世紀的莫爾佛塔
The Mo'er Buddhist Stupa(6th Century A. D.), on the outskirts of old Kashgar.

考察現場
On - site study of tombs.

巴楚出土的唐代大陶缸
Big, Tang Dynasty clay vat unearthed in Bachu.

山普拉出土殉葬的馬及馬鞍彩墊
Remains of sacrificed horse and colored saddle uncovered in
burial site of Shanpula.

公元1世紀普拉墓葬中出土套在絲綢袋中的銅鏡木梳
1st Century copper mirror and wooden comb in silk bag, unearthed from Shanpula burial site.

山普拉墓葬出土的毛織采袋 Colored, woven woolen bag unearthed from Shanpula.

山普拉墓葬出土的蠟染織物 Batik fabric unearthed from Shanpula.

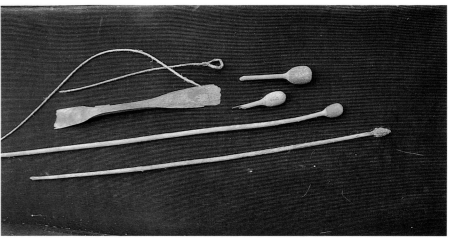

山普拉墓葬出土箭簇 Arrows unearthed from Shanpula.

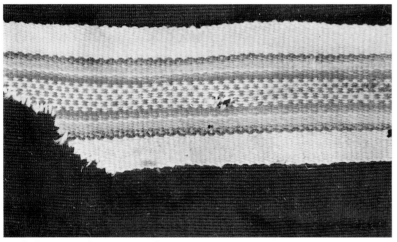

沙漠遺址中出土的毛編彩帶
Woven woolen, colored belt unearthed from Shanpula.

沙漠遺址中出土的絲織殘片
Remnants of silk fabric unearthed from desert ruins.

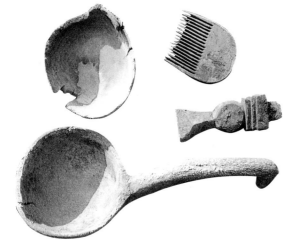

沙漠遺址中出土的木制生活用具
Wooden daily necessities unearthed from desert ruins.

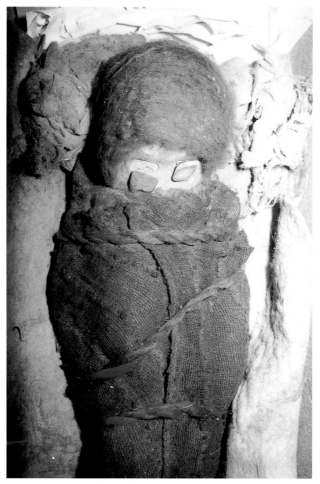

且末縣沙漠墓葬出土的孩童干尸
Dried corpse of a child unearthed from burial site in Qiemo County desert.

山普拉墓葬出土的有漢字絲綢銅鏡袋
Silk sheath for copper mirror with Chinese characters, unearthed from Shanpula.

和田沙漠遺址中出土的有駿馬印記的陶罐把手
Handle of a clay pot with horse seal, unearthed from Hotan desert ruin.

塔克拉瑪干沙漠北緣出土的木雕菩薩像
Carved wooden statue of Buddha unearthed from the northern edge of the Taklimakan Desert.

塔克拉瑪干沙漠北緣出土的木雕菩薩像
Carved wooden statue of Buddha unearthed from the the northern edge of the Taklimakan Desert.

巴楚縣沙漠遺址中出土的塑像
Statue of Bodhisattva unearthed from a desert ruin in Bachu County.

巴楚縣沙漠遺址中出土的佛範
Relief of Bodhisattva unearthed from desert ruin in Bachu County.

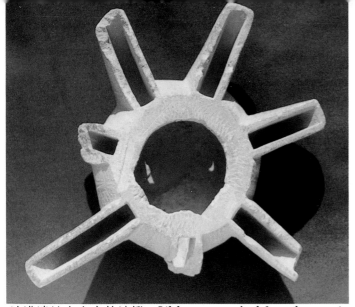

沙漠遺址中出土的油燈　Oil lamp unearthed from desert ruins.

沙漠遺址中出土的唐代(公元6世紀)及喀喇汗王朝(公元10世紀后)錢幣
Tang Dynasty (6th Century) and Karakhanate (late 10th Century) coins
unearthed from desert ruins.

巴楚沙漠遺址中出土的"孝"字銅飾件
Copper ornament with inscription of 'filial piety' unearthed from desert ruin in Bachu.

疏附縣古絲路上烏帕兒鄉出土波斯人頭像、聯珠紋陶殘片
Pottery fragment with continuous bead design and head image
of Persian, unearthed from Wupa on ancient Silk Road in Shufu County.

巴楚沙漠出土的奇特的陶器
Unique pottery unearthed from desert in Bachu.

瓦 石 峽 遺 址

瓦石峽遺址位于若羌縣城西南約 80 公里的瓦石峽鄉，現瓦石峽河南岸 10 公里，古瓦石峽河干河床西約 2 公里處，遺址分布于南北長約 2 公里，東西寬約 1 公里的狹長鹽碱荒漠地帶，由于風沙侵蝕，遺址保存狀況極差，地表遺迹多已無存，已很難讓人想象當時那生機勃勃的綠洲景象。該遺址從公元 4 世紀綿延至公元 14 世紀，即魏晉時期的鄯善國后期開始到宋元時期。

瓦石峽遺址區內共發現三十余處房址，三處窑址，兩處墓地，一處冶鐵遺址，地表散落大量陶片、石磨盤、玻璃片、瓷片、錢幣、坩鍋、絲織品及各種裝飾品和飾件，這些豐富遺物爲我們提供了衆多古文化信息。經考古發掘出土的文物中，有引起衆多學者關注的元代漢文文書和殘玻璃器皿，元代的漢文文書在新疆發現極少，該遺址出土的紙質墨寫的文書，1982 年曾調往北京匯報展出，對元初新疆的歷史起到重要的補證作用。出土的大量殘玻璃器皿更是在新疆古文化遺址中少見，這些玻璃質地較粗劣、熔煉溫度也較低，其工藝技術、造型風格與古代波斯、阿拉伯的玻璃器皿有着相當多的共性，化學成份也相似，可能爲中亞玻璃器的仿制品，對研究西域玻璃生産、玻璃制造技術以及中西交流方面提供了寶貴的實物資料。

（阮秋榮）

The Vash – shahri Site

The Vash – shahri Site is situated at a long and narrow deserted strip of ground, about 2km across from east to west and 2km in length from south to north, around 2km to the west of a dried riverbed of the old Vash – shahri River and 10km to the south of the new Vash – shahri River in Vash – shahri Village, approximately 80km to the southwest of the seat of Ruoqiang County. Being eroded by wind and sand, the site now is in a very bad preservation sitation. There is nearly nothing to be survived on the ground. By these, it is difficult to believe that here was once an oasis full of life. The site had existed here from the 4th c. A. D. to 14th c. A. D., i. e. from the later period of Shanshan kingdom in Wei – Jin times to Song – yuan times.

Altogather 30 dwellings, 3 kilns, 2 cemeteries and an iron smeltery have been found here. Fragments of potteries, stonemills, chinawares, coins, crucible, silk, and other ornaments can be traced to. These relics afford us some ancient cultural informations. Among them the Chinese documents and the glasswares of Yuan Dynasty, which are seldom seen in Xinjiang, secured attention of a lot of scholars. The unearthed paper documents with ink – written characters were once sent to Beijing for exhibition in 1982. All these are great useful to suppling of missing records of the history of Xinjiang in Yuan Dynasty. The glasswares are coarsely made under a rather low temperature. They are similar in technology and style to that of ancient Persian and Arab. So they may be the imitaions of that of Central Asia. However, they supply with valuable materials in kind to the research of the production and making of glass and of the cultural exchanges between China and West.

（Ruan Qiurong）

玉石料珠　Jade beads.

出土的波斯人頭像陶片
Unearthed clay piece with head image of a Persian.

陶坩鍋 Clay crucible.

玻璃器 Glassware

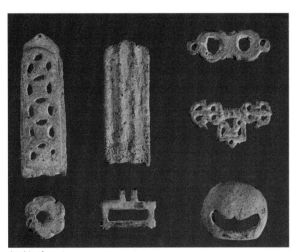
銅飾牌 Copper ornament.

鸭纹铜牌 Duck Pattern bronze plaque

野外考察 Field work.

揭 開 克 里 雅 神 秘 的 面 紗

1993年以來，新疆文物考古研究所與法國科研中心315所合作，先后四次組織考察隊，沿克里雅河深入塔克拉瑪干沙漠中心，全面詳細調查了克里雅河尾閭及其以外的生態環境變遷和古人類活動遺存，逐步揭開了克里雅河神秘的面紗。

克里雅河發源于昆侖山脉，向北流入塔里木盆地中心然后消失于沙漠，漢代時綠洲城國扜彌當此地界。據《漢書》：扜彌國"王治扜彌城……户三千三百四十，口二萬四十，勝兵三千五百四十人。……西通于闐三百九十里。"是當時西域一大國。到漢魏時期，并屬于于闐。扜彌國的位置正好在絲綢之路南道的中段。但關于這樣一個西域古國，却没有可資證明的歷史遺迹被發現，成為一個歷史之謎。

1896年在克里雅河下游三角洲綠洲大河沿西北20余公里的老三角洲上發現了一大片遺址區：喀拉墩遺址群，這是一個結構完整的大型聚落遺址，以喀拉墩古城為中心，四周環繞着十幾處建築群落，寺廟、灌溉渠道、果園和田地。我們對古城、民居和佛寺進行了局部發掘，獲得了一批珍貴文物，為最后解秘該遺址準備了關鍵性的材料。特別是發現了一些精美的壁畫，用綫描畫出人物輪廓，再在適當部位添上適當的顏色，造像面部豐潤，神態端莊自然，給人以清雅脱俗，逼真生動之感。

然而喀拉墩遺址的年代在漢晋時期，不是這個歷史之謎的答案。

然后，激動人心的時刻終于來到了，調查隊在喀拉墩西北40公里的地方找到了更古老的三角洲，在那里意外地新發現了一座古城——圓沙古城。古城呈不規則方形，城墻周長995米，高3—4米，最高達11米，頂部寬3—4米。南面和東面各開一城門。據碳14測定和出土文物推斷，年代上限當不晚于西漢。

此外，在古城周圍及附近還發現了灌溉渠道和6處古墓地。出土陶器有夾砂紅陶和黑陶，器表飾刻劃幾何紋、附加堆紋。另外，石器以及麥、粟、谷物和羊、牛、駱駝等家畜遺骸也有一定量出土。這個新遺址的發現，可能給古扜彌之謎找到了最終的答案，同時也證實了歷史時期以來克里雅河自西向東漂移的論斷，它是環境變遷的主因。

(肖小勇)

Uncover the Secrets of Keriya

In cooperation with UPR – 315, CNRS, Xinjiang Institute of Archaeology have made four investigations to the Keriya River since 1993. Archaeologists passed along the river to go deep into the center of the Taklamakan Desert to investigate completely ancient remains which may be survived there and environmental changes in and beyond the terminals of the river.

The Keriya River rises in the Kunlun Mountains, flows northwards into the Tarim Basin, and disappears in desert. Yu – mi, an oasis town country , is located in this area. According to the Han Annals, Yu – mi kingdom "place its capital at the city of Yu – mi··· (in the kingdom) there are 3340 families, comprising 20040 persons, with 3540 trained troops. towards the west it is distant 390 Li from Yu – tian." It is one of the greatest countries in the Western Regions in that time. During the periods of Han and Wei, it was combined into Yu – tian. Though this kingdom had occupied the center of the southern route of the Silk Road for a certain time, there are nearly nothing to be found concerning it. This remains a mystery.

In 1896, an ancient site, named Kara – dong, was found at an old delta of the Keriya River. It lies more than 20km to the northwest of Da – he – yan at the new delta. Kara – dong Site, taking ancient Kara – dong city surrounded by over 10 groups of residences, shrines, canals, orcharts and farmland, etc. as its center, is a large – scale ancient settlement with complete system. We have made some excavations to the city, a few of houses , and two shrines, and got valuable historical relics which are much benefit for us to open the secrets. The unearthed wall – paintings are especially impor-tant. Ancient artists firstly drew an outline of the figures by skills of line draw, then filled in suitable colour. All the figures are beautifully shaped with plunp and smooth – skinned face and natural expression, and have a sense of elegance and truth.

But the date of them is during Han – Jin times. So it is not the answer.

Then, however, an inspiring time came at last. A new ancient city , named Yuan – sha, was found. It is located at an elder delta 40km to the northwest of Kara – dong. This city is nearly square, with mud – built walls which measured 3 – 4 meters high, the highest reaches to a height of 11 meters with a width of 3 – 4 meters on the top. It has a circumfence of 995 meters. A gate is made on the south, the other one on the east . According to radio carbon dating and the unearthed relics, the date of the city goes back to a period before the Western Han Dynasty.

At the surroundings there found a canal and six cemeteries of ancient times. Potteries unearthed from the cemeteries are hand – made, red or black , on outer surface incised geometric figures and attached other de-signs. Besides, there also found a certain number of stonewares, wheat, millet and other crops, and skeletons of sheep, cow and camel. Perhaps this new discovery of the site is the final answer of the secret. In the meantime, it proves that the Keriya River was drifted towards east from west, which be-came a key cause of the environmental changes of the river.

(Xiao Xiaoyong)

散落在地面的破陶罐
Broken pottery jug scattered on the ground

佛像
Buddha

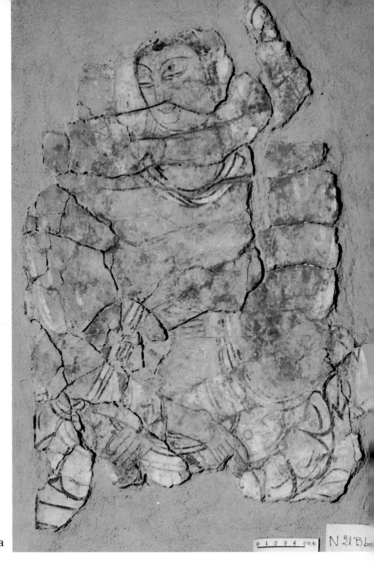

佛像
Buddha

采集標本
Collecting speciments

調查隊員在途中午餐
The investigation members are at lunch on the way

覩貨邏故國——安迪爾遺址

公元 645 年，西天取經歸來的唐僧玄奘沿沙漠南道東行，出尼壤城后他寫道："行四百余里，至覩貨邏故國。國久空曠，城皆荒蕪。"據考證，此空國荒城，就在今安迪爾遺址。

安迪爾遺址位于今安迪爾牧場東南 20 余公里、安迪爾河東岸的沙漠中，西距民豐縣城 130 余公里，是絲路南道上著名而重要的古址。騎駱駝自牧場前去探訪，當天便能返回。

首先映入眼簾的是一座佛塔，它高達 7 米，用土坯築就，分塔基與塔身兩部分。塔基方形，分三層，最底層最大，邊長約 8.2 米。塔基總高 2.7 米。塔身圓柱形，直徑 4.9 米，高 4.3 米。頂作覆鉢形。考慮到經年的風蝕，原來應更高些。

安迪爾遺址範圍相當廣闊，方圓達十幾平方公里，在密密麻麻散布着各種古代遺物的地域里，坐落着兩座古城遺址。本世紀初，英國探險家斯坦因曾兩度前來考察和挖掘，有過驚人的發現。

其一在佛塔東南約 1.5 公里。城牆尚在，圓形，城門南開，上有門樓。城牆泥築，最高達 7 米。古城直徑約 130 米。城中央建寺廟與規模宏大的官署。寺廟土木結構，內牆邊長 5.5 米，內殿四角置蓮花座，上立四天王塑像，中央是八角形大臺基，上立真人大小的灰泥雕像，在這里出土了大量文書，其中有陀羅尼經、舍利犖坦摩經。漢語文書中提到了"左羽林軍大將軍王直將"，西牆上書漢文題記，明確提到"四鎮"、"大蕃"及其官員和"太常卿秦嘉興歸本道"字樣，落款是唐開元七年，即公元 719 年。另外還發現許多藏文題字。寺廟北房中牆壁上還殘留有壁畫、繪佛和菩薩像。可以推定，該城當廢弃于公元 8 世紀以后，顯然不會是玄奘的"荒城"。

另一座位于佛塔東北，城牆已風蝕幾盡，只剩下一段土坯加泥土叠壘而成的土丘，將它們連接起來，才大致可看出這是一座近似于方形的橢圓形古城，樣子十分古老。城牆內約略可見出街道與房舍的基礎，陶片十分密集，還撿到一枚漢佉二體錢。其時代應當在 4 世紀前后。玄奘的"荒城"，可能即在此。

不過，漢文史籍中，南道諸國中從未提到"覩貨邏"。而玄奘眼見時卻又故去了。這段歷史的插曲到底應該如何解釋，看來只能留待以后了。

(肖小勇)

官署
Government office

佛塔
Stupa

Old Tu – huo – luo Country—the Ancient Site of Endere

Xuan Zang, the great monk of the Tang Dynasty, who passed along the desert route of the south on his return journey from the Western Paradise about A. D. 645, wrote that after leaving the city of Ni – rang, i. e. the Niya Site, "For over 400 Li, arrived at the old Tu – huo – luo country. The country had been emptied for a long time , and the cities all wasted." According to texture research , this emptied country and its wasted cities were identified with the ancient site of Endere.

The ancient site of Endere , which is located in desert near the eastern bank of the Endere River, over 20km to the southeast of Endere Village and more than 130km westwards to the county town of Mingfeng, is a well – known important ancient site on the Silk Road. To visit the site by camel from the village, you can come back in the same day.

The first thing coming into view is a Buddhist stupa, measuring to 7m high. It was built with sun – dried bricks, including two parts: the base and the body. The base, which is square, rises in three stories to a height of 2. 7m, of which the lowest is about 8. 2 meters square. The body has a cylindrical dome resting on a drum, measuring 4. 3m high and 4. 9m in diameter. Considering having been wind – eroded for years, the original height should be a little biger.

This site covers an area of over 10 square kilometers. Within a closely dotted miscelaneous relics – scattered place stand two ancient cities. In the early part of this century, Aurel Stein, a British explorer, had ever come here twice to investigate and excavate the site and got astonishing finds.

One of the cities lies about 1. 5km to the southeast of the stupa, which was built in a round, measuring about 130m in diameter, with mud – built city walls still rising to a height of 7m. In the southern wall is opened a gate over which stands a gatehouse. In the center of the city is a shrine and a government office on a grand scale. The shrine is built of clay and woods.

The inside of it measured 5. 5 meters square. In the four corners of the cella are placed lotus seats on which stand sculptures of the Four Devaguardians. The octagonal base in the center of the cella was once occupied by a colossal statue made of stucco, which probably represented a Buddha. Quantities of documents are found here. Among them are Buddhist texts "Dharani" and "Salistamba – sutra". A Chinese document mentions a general named Wang Zhi: "左羽林軍大將軍王直將". There are Chinese inscriptions on the western wall, which clearly mention the "Four Garrisons", "Great Tibet" and their officials, and the characters "太常卿秦嘉興歸本道". All these were written in the 7th year of Kaiyuan of Tang Dynasty, i. e. A. D. 719. In addition, many Tibetan inscriptions are also found here. On the walls of the northern room in the shrine there remained some wall – paintings with images of Buddha and Bodhisattva. So it can be concluded that this city was abandoned in the 8th century A. D. and it is obviously not the Xuan Zang's "wasted city".

The other one is situated to the northeast of the stupa, which looks like very old, with seriously eroded city walls. We made out it only by connecting the mounds of soil and sun – dried bricks. This is an oval city similar to square. Inside it are scattered closely pottery fragments. Some traces of street and room can be recognized. A Sino – Kharosthi coin is found here, which can go back to about the 4th century A. D. . One of the "wasted cities" of Xuan Zang's probably is this.

However, the other Chinese historical books don't mention the country Tu – huo – luo on the route of south. But Xuan Zang exactly wrote that it was between Niya and Qiemo and abandoned before his arrival. To explain this need further materials. So I have to leave it over.

(Xiao Xiaoyong)

覩貨邏故國——安迪爾遺址

漢佉二體錢
Sino - Kharosthi coin

木雕菩薩像
Wooden Bodhisattva

Old Tu – huo – luo Country—the Ancient Site of Endere

絲路考古的驚人發現——新疆營盤第 15 號墓

漢晋時期是西域文明史的輝煌時期。絲綢之路的開闢，爲東西方文化藝術在這片亞洲腹心區域的匯聚交流創造了條件。

1995 年秋季，新疆的考古工作者在樓蘭故城西近 200 公里的營盤搶救性發掘了一批漢晋時期墓葬，有來自中原地區色彩絢麗的錦、綉、漆器，更有中亞、西亞特色的彩色毛織物。1997 年 5 月開啓的第 15 號木棺及隨葬品最爲引人矚目。

棺外覆蓋彩色獅紋栽絨毯，棺四壁及棺蓋滿繪圓圈、菱格、卷草、花卉等圖案。棺內葬一男性個體，仰身直肢，身材高大，約 1.8 米以上。他身蓋素絹衾，面罩麻質人面形面具，表情溫厚、安詳、栩栩如生；穿著紅底對人獸樹紋罽袍、素絹貼金內袍、菱紋四瓣花毛綉長褲、絹面貼金氈靴。這些服飾織綉圖案精美富麗，構思新穎奇妙，令人稱絶；僅此一墓，所出規格甚高的葬具、衣物、殉品，不僅在新疆甚至國內都極爲罕見。其中對人獸樹紋罽袍堪稱世界文物奇品，爲雙層兩面紋織物，這種雙層毛織物爲唐代及其后我國內地雙層絲織物的産生開了先河。袍面紋樣設計規整，每區由六組以石榴樹爲軸兩兩相對的人物、動物組成，每組以二方連續形式橫貫終幅。人物有四組，形象一致，均男性、裸體、卷髮、高鼻、大眼。各組人物姿態各异，手中分別持矛、盾、劍之類兵器，兩兩相對，表現出不同的對練姿態，細致、生動。它體現着希臘文化藝術的風格，是一千七八百年前，織工用毛紗一梭一梭織出來的。

從這件罽袍的織造工藝、紋樣風格可以斷定，它是通過絲綢之路由中亞、西亞一帶輸入我國西域的毛織物精品，穿著它的墓主人很可能是一位來自西方從事貿易的富商。

營盤是漢晋時期塔里木河、孔雀河下游一處地理位置十分重要的古代聚落，營盤墓葬的考古收獲生動地再現了營盤作爲交通重鎮在當時絲路貿易、東西文化交流等方面所具有的重要地位。

(李文瑛)

紅地"登高"錦
Brocade with characters "登高" on red ground

Astonishing Archaeological Finds of the Silk Road
——the Tomb 15 of Ying – pan in Xinjiang

The period of Han and Jin is a splendid historical stage of the civilizations of the Western Regions. With opening of the Silk Road, cultures and arts from both East and West exchanged and gathered togather here.

In autumn, 1995, Xinjiang archaeologists excavated large numbers of tombs of Han – Jin times at Ying – pan, nearly 200km to the west of the ancient Loulan City. Numerous objects were found there. Among them, some are bright-coloured brocade, embroidery, and lacquerwares from the Central Plains of China, and some are colourful woollens in Central and Western Asian style. The wooden coffin No. 15, opened in May, 1997, and its burial articles are the most noticeable.

The coffin, of which the four side panels and the ladger are painted with colourful designs of circles, lozenged – checks, curled – up plants and flowers, is covered with a colourful blanket with a lion motif. Within the coffin a male corpse, in a height of over 1. 8m, lying straight supine, is found. He is covered on body with a white Juan silk quilt and on face with a male face like linen mask. He is dressed in a gold foil white Juan silk underwear which is covered with a red woolen robe with designs of paired human figures, animals and trees, a long woolen pants with embroidered rohombic grids and four – petal flowers patterns, and a pair of felt boots with a gold foil Juan silk cover. These clothes are elegantly embroidered in patterns in a novel style. The coffin, artcles of clothing, and sacrificial objects from the tomb are seldom seen not only in Xinjiang but in the whole country. The woolen robe of double – layer can be rated as a gem in the world. It becomes the origin of double – layer silk of Tang Dynasty and later on. The robe has a regular pattern which is separated into divisions. Each divisions consists of over six sets of figures and animals facing each other in twos and twos and with a pomegranate as the middle shaft. Each set takes the form of two continual squares till the end of the entire piece. There are four sets of figures with similar images, male, nude, with curly hair, high nose and big eyes. These figures, in various postures, with spear, shield or sword in their hands, face to face in twos and twos, carefully and lively show different carriages of practising martial arts facing each other. These were woven by weavers with woolen yarn 1700 – 1800 years ago, presenting a Greek artistic style.

To judge from the weaving skill and the style of patterns of the robe, it can be concluded that it was imported from Central and Western Asia through the Silk Road, and the occupant of the tomb, who was in the robe, perhaps was a rich businessman from the West.

Ying – pan was an important ancient settlement at the lower reaches of the Tarim River and the Kongque River in the periods of Han and Jin. The archaeological finds of the Ying – pan Cemetery lively reappear the important position of Ying – pan as a traffic hub in the trade and cultural exchanges between East and West through the Silk Road in that time.

(Li Wenying)

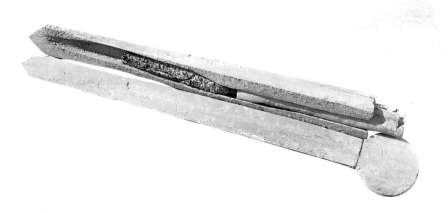

冥衣
Funerary cloth

鐵刀
Iron knife

營盤男尸
Male mummy of Yingpan

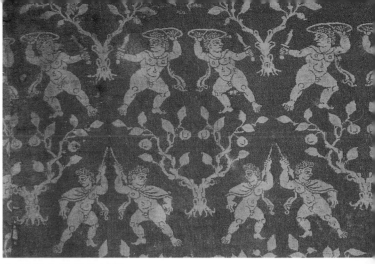

紅地對人獸樹紋罽袍
Woolen robe with paired human figures, animales and trees design on red ground

絹面貼金氈靴
Felt boots with gold foil and juan silk vamp

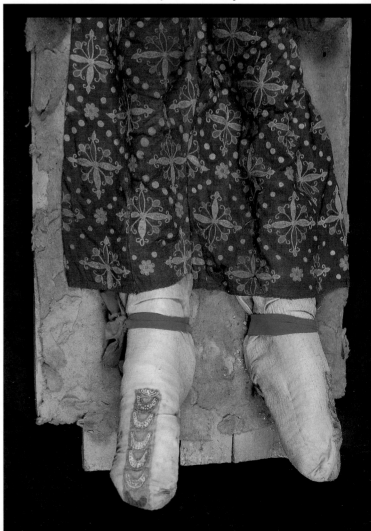

塔克拉玛干三大故城

探險丹丹烏里克

丹丹烏里克位于一沙山環繞的狹長地帶，干涸的古河道自南向北貫穿而過。遺跡沿河分布，東西寬約 2 公里，南北綿延十余公里。重要遺跡集中在南部，包括圓形城堡、民居、寺廟在內，共發現近 20 處建築群廢墟，它們與古灌溉渠道、果園、田地一道，構成一個統一的結構完整的聚落遺址。

強勁的沙漠風和流動沙丘，至今仍是遺址面臨的主要威脅，許多建築物已被侵蝕殆盡。

寺廟建築占相當比重，在發現的不到 20 處建築群中，有將近一半是或含有佛教寺廟。其中還有一處漢僧寺院——護國寺。寺廟裝飾着與大乘佛教有關的雕塑與壁畫，人物造形主要有佛、菩薩、乾達婆、供養人等，還有其他表示佛教故事的壁畫。

建築多爲木框架結構，墻心以樹枝和葦草編栅構成，兩面涂拌膠泥。一處建築群一般包括大廳、卧房、伙房、雜房、畜欄、院子、栅欄及四周之果園、有的還附有寺院。

出土文物除石、陶、銅、鐵、玻璃、錢幣外，還有大量的板畫，它們有的涉及到一些著名的傳奇故事和各類文書，涉及漢、梵、婆邏迷等不同語種，內容從官方文牒到普通信函，從契約到佛教典籍，相當廣泛。從這些文書中我們得知，遺址大約廢弃于公元 8 世紀末期，本名叫犂謝或犂謝鎮，一個叫楊晋卿的將軍作過它的知鎮官。它的上級部門是"六城"，長官是質邏刺史阿摩支尉遲。這些都是唐代史籍中所沒有的珍貴材料。

然而我們至今没有直接的考古證據來證明遺址的廢弃到底因于何種原因，就把它作爲一個歷史的懸念，留給人們去猜測，去想往，去探索吧！

(肖小勇)

Explore Dandan—Uiliq

Dandan – Uiliq is situated at a long and narrow strip of ground surrounded by sand – dunes. A dried ancient river course cuts through the site from south to north. The remains, which are scattered along the course, extend over 10km from south to north. The important ones are all at the south, including a circumvallation, dwellings, shrines, etc., totaling nearly 20 groups of ruins of structures. Togather with ancient canals, orcharts, and farmland, the Dandan – Uiliq Site forms a completed settlement.

This site is being faced with a serious imperilling of strong desert wind and drifting sand. Many structures have been eroded.

The proportion of shrines in the site is very big. Among the discovered less than 20 groups of ruins of structures nearly a half are or contain shrines. Among them there is a Chinese monk shrine named Hu – luo – si. The shrines are decorated with wall – paintings and sculptures concerning Mahayana Buddhism. Images of Buddha, Bodhisattva, Gandharva can be recognized. There are also other scenes showing Buddhist stories in the wall – paintings.

The structures have a stucture of wooden frame, taking railings of reeds and twigs as cores of the wall, surfaces of the wall coated with stucco. A structure generally consists of a main room, bedroom, kitchen, livestock shed, yard, fences, sometime and a shrine.

Besides objects of stone, pottery, bronze, iron and glass and coins, there remained a large number of painted panels dealing with some well – known Buddhist legends, and various documents of different languages, such as Chinese, Sanskrit and Brahmi, etc., including official dispatches, common letters, deeds, and Buddhist texts. They show us that the site of Dandan – Uiliq was abandoned at the close of the eighth century, its original name was Li – xie or Li – xie town, a general, named Yang Jinqing, had once been the commandant of it, and Li – xie belonged to an administrative division, named Liu – cheng, of which the Zhi – luo prefect and A – mo – zhi named Wei – chi. All these are precious historical materials never seen in history of Tang Dynasty.

But up to now no immediate archaeological evidence can explain why the site was deserted. In that case, let's leave it to the future. One interested in it can guess, can probe, and can prove this historical secret.

(Xiao Xiaoyong)

浮雕菩薩

A relief sculpture of Bodhisattva

板畫

Wooden panel bearing paintings

板畫"蠶種西傳"

Wooden panel bearing paintings of "Silk – bringing Princess"

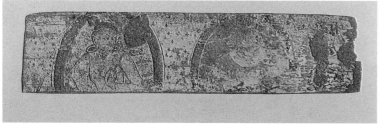

板畫"聖鼠崇拜"的故事

Wooden panel bearing paintings of "the Sacred Rats"

不同規格的銅錢
Various copper coins

殘陶罐
Broken pottery jug

樓　　蘭

樓蘭遺址位于新疆巴音郭楞蒙古自治州若羌縣羅布泊沿岸，地理坐標爲東經 89°55′22″、北緯 40°29′55″，地處塔里木盆地最低窪地區。現今這里大部分已爲無情的流沙所湮没，受風力侵蝕形成獨特的"雅丹"地貌，歷史上受塔里木河和孔雀河的恩賜，形成一片廣闊的河流冲積平原，加之地處中西交通咽喉，使其成爲"絲綢之路"上的一顆閃亮明珠。

1900 年瑞典人斯文·赫定首次發現樓蘭遺址，這一發現揭開了塔克拉瑪干沙漠探險的序幕，曾被譽爲是"中世紀文明的曙光"，1980 年在羅布泊孔雀河下游的鐵板河三角洲地區出土了一具保存完好的女尸，被世人稱爲"樓蘭美女"，震驚國内外，掀起了絲路考古的熱潮。樓蘭古城的面積達 10 萬平方米，城中有官署、民居、佛寺塔廟等遺迹，城郊有干涸的古河道、水渠田陌遺址，城北面分布有古墓群、佛塔、烽燧等。整個遺址區出土了大量漢文和佉盧文木簡文書、漢代錢幣、銅鏡、一枚貴霜錢幣、華麗的漢代漆器、絲毛織品、精致的木陶雕刻器皿等文物。織造精美的東漢織錦如"延年益壽大宜子孫錦"、"永昌錦"、"長壽光明錦"、"長

樂光明錦"等，在繁縟的流雲攀枝卷葉紋和祥禽瑞獸紋中夾織吉祥語，實屬罕見珍品；出土的魏晉時期漢文木簡反映了當時西域長史府屯田官兵的社會政治生産活動；佉盧文則反映了鄯善國時期的社會面貌；衆多的文物透視着中西文化、物質交流的頻繁。

樓蘭，史載爲西漢西域三十六國之一，東漢時成爲西域長史府所在地，后爲鄯善國所并，因位于塔里木盆地東部，成爲中原通西域最便捷的通道。作爲當時西域政治、經濟、交通的樞紐，樓蘭曾輝煌昌盛一時，但東漢以后即隱没于史籍記載，公元 4 世紀末已人去城空田地荒蕪，"上無飛鳥，下無走獸"，被廢弃的最基本原因是孔雀河水的改道，致使下游地區水源枯竭。因此樓蘭遺址出土的各類文物，特别是木簡文書，不僅彌補了史籍記載的缺乏，更有助于我們進一步揭示古樓蘭國的古代文明。

(阮秋榮)

樓蘭古城遺址
Ancient city of Loulan

Loulan Site

The Loulan Site is located at longitude 89°55'55"east, latitude 40°29'22"north, near Lopnor, the lowest place in the Tarim Basin, in Ruoqiang County, Bayinkolen Monggol Autonomous Prefecture, Xinjiang. Most of Lopnor now is covered by drifting sand or eroded into peculiar"Yardang" by wind. But in history, by feeding of the Tarim River and Kongque River, here was a vast alluvial plain and was a cross–roads between China and West. And the Loulan became a bright pearl on the "Silk Road".

The Loulan Site was firstly found by Sven Hedin, a Swede, in 1900. It opened the prelude of explorations in the Taklamakan Desert and was well–known as the"dawn of civilizations of the Middle Ages". In 1980, a well–preserved female mummy was unearthed at the delta of the Tieban River at the lower reaches of the Kongque River, near Lopnor, who was afterwards called "Loulan beauty". This astonishing discovery started a new upsurge of archaeology of the Silk Road. Ancient Loulan City covers an area of 100,000 square meters. Within it there are remains of a government office, dwellings, shrines and stupas, etc.. Out of it some dried ancient river course, canals and farmlands can be traced. To the north of the city, ancient tombs, stupas and beacon towers are distributed over. Quantities of relics have been excavated there, including quantities of Chinese and Kharosthi documents, coins, bronze mirrows, a Kusana coin, gorgeous lacquerwares and silk and woolen fabrics, and fine wooden and pottery sculptures, etc.. Beautiful brocades of the Eastem Han always have overelaborate designs of flowing clouds, climbing twigs, rolling leaves, and lucky animals. Among the designs the brocades are still woven with propitious words, such as "延年益壽大宜子孫", "永昌", "長壽光明", "長樂光明", etc.. The Chinese documents show some political, social and productive activities of the garrison troops of the Zhangshi prefecture of the Western Regions of that time, and the Kharosthi tablets reflect the social conditions of Shanshan Kingdom. Large numbers of the relics present the frequent cultural and material exchanges between China and west.

In historical records, Loulan was one of the 36 kingdoms in the Western Regions in the Western Han times. During the Eastern Han Dynasty, it became the seat of the Zhang–shi Prefecture of the Western Regions, and soon after that it was combined into Shanshan kingdom. Being situated at the east of the Tarim Basin, Loulan had once been a hub connecting the Central Plains and the Western Regions, and had had splendid history. But after the Eastern Han, it disapeared in the history. To the close of the 4th century, there was nothing survived but the emptied city and the wasted land, "no a bird in the sky, and no an animal on the ground."The most essential cause of the abandonment of the site is that the Kongque River changed its course in that time, and as a result, the source of water of this region dried up, then the site of ancient Loulan was abandoned. These unearthed relics, especially the wooden documents, can not only make up the loss of the history, but also help us bring to light the ancient civilizations of the Loulan kingdom.

(Ruan Qiurong)

海頭古城
Ancient city of Haitou

L.L. 古城
Ancient city L.L.

石器
Stonewares

官署
Government office

石磨
Millstones

全国重点文物保护单位

楼蘭故城遺址
ANCIENT CITY RUIN OF LOLAN

一串料珠
A string of glassbeads

海頭古城
Ancient city of Haitou

樓蘭古城內西北民居建築一角
A corner of the dwellings in northwest of the ancient Loulan city

"延年益壽 大宜子孫"錦
Brocade with characters "延年益壽 大宜子孫"

楼兰佛塔
Stupa of Loulan site

漢文文書
Chinese ducuments

漢文木簡
Wooden slips with Chinese characters

漆杯
Lacquer cup

樓蘭官署遺址
Remains of government office of Loulan

彩色毛毯　Colour blanket

紅地"登高"錦
Brocade with characters "登高" on red ground

漆蓋
Lacquer lid

押花銅戒指
Signet – rings

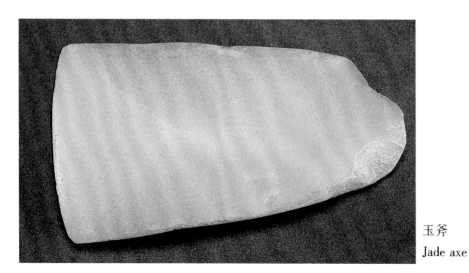

玉斧
Jade axe

貴霜錢幣
A coin of Kusana

尼 雅 遺 址

尼雅遺址是漢晉時期西域"絲綢之路"南道上的一處東西交通要塞，位於新疆和田地區民豐縣以北約100公里的塔克拉瑪干沙漠南緣，尼雅河下游尾閭地帶。遺址以北緯37°58′45.3″，東經82°43′13.5″的佛塔爲中心，沿古尼雅河道呈南北向帶狀分布，分布範圍南北長約30公里，東西寬約7公里，其間散落房屋居址、佛塔、寺院、城址、冶鑄遺址、陶窑、墓葬、果園、水渠、潟壩等各種遺迹約百余處，是新疆古文化遺址中規模最大且保存狀況良好又極具學術研究價值的大型遺址之一。

從1901年英籍匈牙利人馬克·奧里爾·斯坦因首次發現尼雅遺址到近年的中日尼雅遺址聯合學術考察，尼雅考古已走過了近百年歷程，特別是近年的中日聯合考察，對該遺址進行了系統調查和科學規範的考古發掘，發現了許多重要古文化遺存和珍貴遺物，逐漸揭開了尼雅遺址神秘的面紗。

1995年尼雅I號墓地的發現，使尼雅考古獲得豐碩成果，被國家文物局評爲當年"全國十大考古發現之一"，轟動學術界，使尼雅遺址備受世人矚目。在100平方米範圍内共發掘了8座屬社會上層統治集團的墓葬，隨葬品豐富，級別高，保存完好。按其種類可分爲陶器、木器、鐵器、漆器、弓矢、紡織品及料珠等，其中紡織品爲其大宗，特別是出土了一批組織復雜、色彩絢爛、花紋繁縟的絲織品和精美毛織品，如被國家文物局鑒定委員會定爲國寶級文物的"王侯合昏千秋萬歲宜子孫"錦衾，"五星出東方利中國"錦護膊，還有"延年益壽長保子孫"、"世毋極錦宜二親傳子孫"、"登高明望四海貴富壽爲國慶"、"金池鳳"等華麗織錦，色彩斑爛，保存之佳實屬空前罕見。

尼雅遺址是《漢書·西域傳》中記載的"精絶"國故址，東漢后期爲鄯善所并，后受魏晉王朝節制。因其地處絲路南道交通必經之地，大量文物的出土不僅反映了濃郁的地域文化特色，更爲研究西域史、絲綢之路史、古代東西文化交流史提供了翔實資料。

（阮秋榮）

Niya Site

Located at the end of the Niya River, on the southern fringe of the Taklamakan Desert, about 100km to the north of Mingfeng County, Hetian Prefecture, Xinjiang, Niya site was a cross – roads between East and West for communication on the southern route of the "Silk Road" in the Western Regions in Han – Jin times. Taking a stupa, at Longitude 82°43′33.5″E, Latitude 37°58′45.3″N, as the center, it is distributed along an ancient course of the Niya River, covering 30km in length from south to north and about 7km across from east to west. Within the area over 100 remains are scattered, including dwellings, stupas, shrines, city, smeltery, pottery kilns, tombs, orcharts, canals, and water – tanks etc.. The Niya site is one of the largest well – preserved historical sites in Xinjiang and is of great academic value.

From its first discovery by Aurel Stein in 1901 to the Sino – Japan joint academic investigations in recent years, Niya archaeology has gone through a course of near 100 years. Systemic investigations and scientific excavations were made to it by Sino – Japan joint exploration party in recent years and quantities of cultural relics were found. The mysterious veil of the Niya Site is gradually uncovered.

One of the most important finds is the cemetery 1, which was excavated in 1995 and rated as one of the "ten most major archaeological finds of the nation"by the State Cultural Relics Bureau in the same year. Within an area of 100 square meters, 8 tombs of upper classes of society were excavated, from which large numbers of well – preserved high – level burial articles were unearthed. They include potteries, wooden wares, ironwares, lacquerwares, bow and arrows, textiles, and beads, etc.. The most is textiles. Among them are colourful silk and woolen fabrics with overelaborate designs and Chinese characters , such as the brocade quilt with characters "王侯合昏千秋萬歲宜子孫" and the brocade arm protector with characters"五星出東方利中國", which were fixed as national treasures, and the other brocades with characters "延年益壽長保子孫"，"世毋極錦宜二親傳子孫"，"登高明望四海貴富壽爲國慶"，or"金池鳳" etc.. All these are seldom seen in the world.

The Niya Site was identified with the kingdom of "Jing – jue"in the Han Annals. In later period of the Eastern Han, the kingdom of"Jing – jue" was combined into Shanshan, then was controled by Wei and Jin Dynasties. Because it occupied the only place one must pass through on the southern route of the Silk Road, most unearthed relics of it have both the local cultural features and non – local cultural influence. They afford us full and accurate materials to research the history of the Western Regions, the Silk Road, and of the cultural exchanges between East and West.

（Ruan Qiurong）

荒漠中的"精絕"古國遺址
Ruins of ancient "Jingjue" kingdom in desert

尼雅—古橋遺址
Foot – bridge, Niya Site

尼雅 N7 遺址
Ruined house N. 7, Niya Site

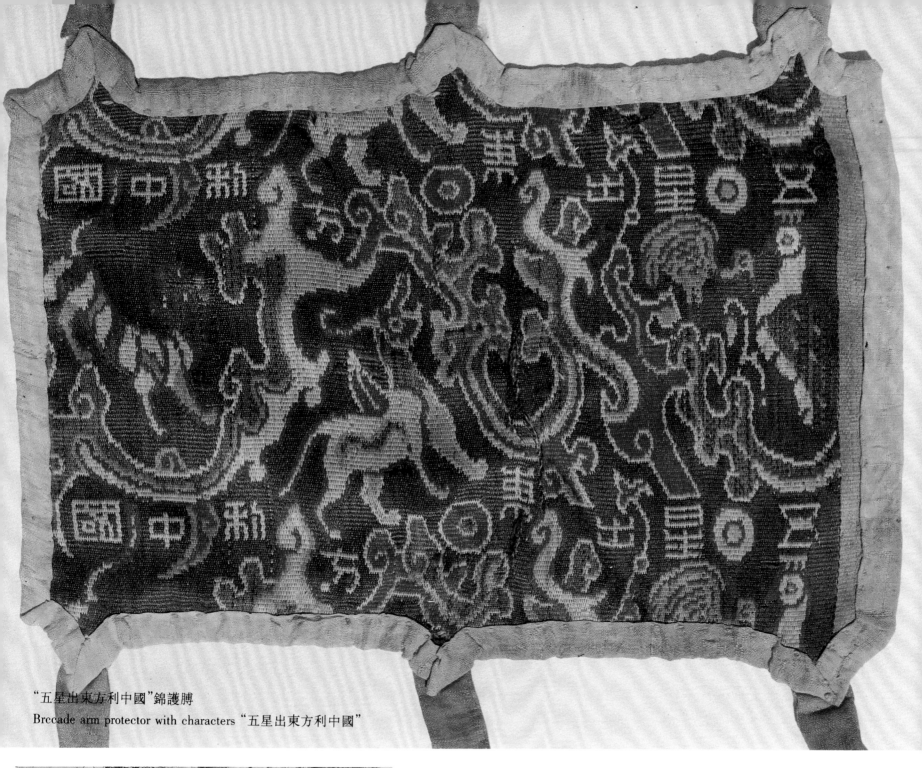

"五星出東方利中國"錦護膊

Brocade arm protector with characters "五星出東方利中國"

尼雅 N2 遺址
Dwellings N. 2, Niya Site

尼雅 N8 遺址
Ruined house N. 8, Niya Site

尼雅佛塔遺址
Ruined stupa, Niya Site

日本佛學人員在佛塔前做佛事
Japanese Buddhists are doing Buddhist service

尼雅 N5 佛寺遺址
Ruined shrine N. 5, Niya Site

佛像（N5 佛寺遺址出土）
Image of Buddha(from N5)

佉盧文木牘
Wooden tablets in Kharosthi

尼雅一號墓地 M8 開棺現場
The scene of coffin's opening of M8, Cemetery 1, Niya Site

尼雅一號墓地 M3 男女主人
Occupants of M3, Cemetery 1, Niya Site

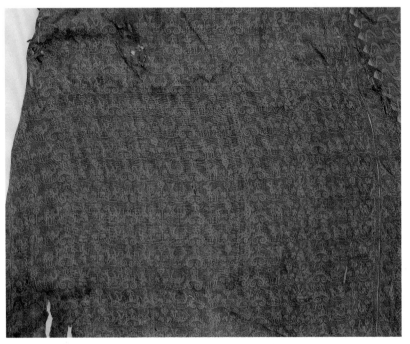

M3 女主人錦袍局部
Part of the brocade robe of the female occupant of M3

弓、箭和箭服
Bow, arrows and arrow quivers

"王"字陶罐
Pottery jug with character "王"

尼雅 N4 遺址附近的木棺
Wooden coffin unearthed near N. 4, Niya Site

"王候合昏千秋萬歲宜于孫"錦衾
Brocade quilt with characters "王候合昏千秋萬歲宜子孫"

漆奩
Lacquer toilet box

綴絹飾暈繝緙花毛袋
Woolen bag with silk decoration

漆奩内的物品
Toilet articles in the lacquer toilet box

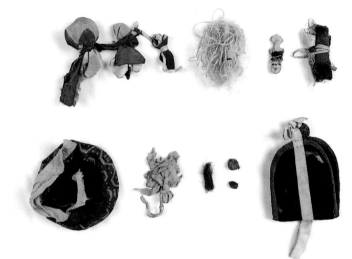

"金池鳳"錦袋
Brocade bag with characters"金池鳳"

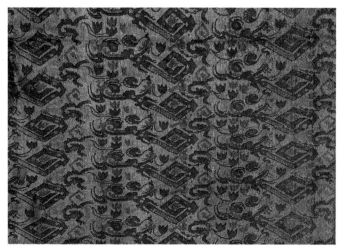

茱萸回文錦覆面局部
Part of the brocade face cover with
dogwood and square spiral design

銅鏡
Bronze mirrow

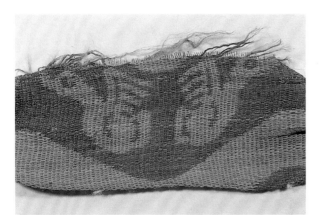

雁紋錦

Brocade with a design of wild geese

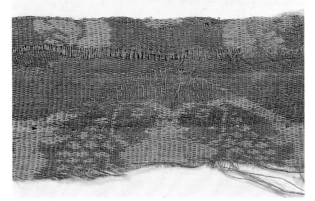

魚紋錦

Brocade with a design of fishes

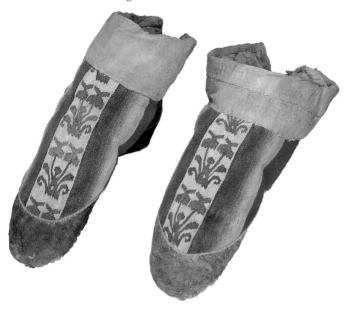

絳地絲履

Silk shoes with designs on crimson ground

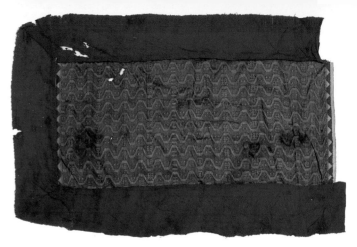

"世毋極錦宜二親傳子孫"錦覆面

Brocade face cover with characters "世毋極錦宜二親傳子孫"

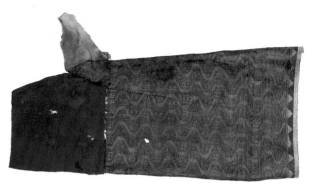

"世毋極錦宜二親傳子孫"錦手套

Brocade gloves with characters "世毋極錦宜二親傳子孫"

茱萸回紋錦覆面

Brocade face cover with dogwood and square spiral design

沙 生 植 物 的 王 國

塔里木盆地也是世界上少有的沙生植物園。除了沿着各條沙漠河兩岸生長着千里胡楊林,在曠漠的大地上,特別是沙漠和綠洲之間還有不少沙生植物維系着盆地的生態平衡。它們各以自己抗御干旱、鹽碱、風沙的特殊生存方式仡立于這片常常受風沙侵襲的大地之上;并一代又一代地把自己的種子借助于漠風、洪水、飛禽撒播到四面八方,哪怕只有千分之一、萬分之一的成活機會也在所不惜。

沙生植物有着有趣而頑強的生長特性。

在塔里木,胡楊是最高大而又生長面積最廣的喬木,約有 450 多萬畝。它是一種古老的樹種,在沙漠中有它,在鹽碱地上有它,因此形成了在惡劣環境下生長、繁衍的特殊本領。從生態上講,胡楊有三奇:奇异的葉型,奇特的生理功能,奇妙的繁育方式。胡楊的幼樹一般都是綫型葉,這是爲了根系發展而節約水份蒸發。一旦根系發育開始吸收地下水份,便在樹冠長出掌型葉以促成樹身迅速上長,所以發它根深之際,也是葉大葉茂之時。這也是一棵成年樹身往往長着三種葉型的原因。胡楊成樹以后不但有强大的吸水性,而且在重鹽碱地上能够通過自身把鹽碱排出,這是它能在鹽碱地上生育發展的一個秘密。胡楊的繁育方式也很特別,最奇妙的是爲了在干旱區利用洪水撒種發芽,種子的成熟期幾乎同塔里木河的洪水泛濫期相吻合;當出現干旱缺水時,它還能通過根系和樹干發出新芽繁衍后代。據在千年以上的沙化地帶和古城遺址考證,那里的許多老胡楊尚未死去,所以人們稱贊胡楊千年不死,死后千年不倒,倒后千年不朽。

被人們稱爲固沙勇士的紅柳今天在塔里木盆地有上千萬畝。這種固沙植物的種子,當它在荒漠中剛剛扎下根來,就通過幼小的身軀開始把流沙集攏在身旁,經過十年、二十年,隨着自身軀干的成長便用那發達的根系把流沙堆積成一座座沙包,形成丘陵似的紅柳叢生的壁壘;春末夏初在那迷蒙的風沙中,紅柳便以粉紅色的花卉點綴着每一沙包的頂部,花期一直開到深秋。

具有防沙籬笆之稱的沙拐棗,帶刺的身軀、濃密的枝葉像一道低矮的林墻減弱着風沙的肆虐,而在深秋又以帶着薄殼的種子滾動在茫茫沙野,尋找自己發芽生根的際遇。

富有詩意的羅布麻,垂墜的花卉像挂滿了粉紅色的鈴鐺,給沙漠邊緣、塔里木河兩岸抹上了淡淡的紅輝。而到深秋,當它的豆夾似的種囊剛剛開裂的時候,那長着細絨毛般翅膀的種子就開始飄揚,像蒲公英般輕柔,落地之后利用土地的濕氣先扎下根,爾后等待來年的成長,由于它枝干柔韌,在漠風中具有枝可屈而不折的特性,因此,它的外衣便成爲其他麻類不可比的最佳麻紡原料。

塔里木盆地,乃至塔克拉瑪干沙海中,也還有蘆葦、芨芨草以及被稱爲沙漠蜜糖的駱駝刺,藥用價值很高的肉蓯蓉、甘草、麻黃草、地老鼠瓜,他們不但具有很强的防風固沙能力,而且也有很高的經濟價值,正是這些高矮、疏密不同的沙生植物,構成了防風治沙、抗御鹽碱的群落。據統計塔里木盆地約有二百多種固沙植物,其中灌木、半灌木約一百種,其余都是多年或一年生草本植物。爲了研究這些植物的生態規律和經濟利用價值,在塔克拉瑪干沙漠南緣流沙活動頻繁的策勒綠洲,科研部門建立起了沙漠研究站,通過多年的研究試驗,不僅培育了大量沙生植物,還通過在沙漠前沿種植,取得了防風固沙的數據。

KINGDOM OF DESERT PLANTS

The Tarim Basin is a rare botanical garden of desert plants. In addition to the thousand – mile diversi – form leaved poplar forests that line the shores of all the rivers in the desert, there are various other desert plants growing between the desert and the oases which help to maintain the ecological balance of the basin. These plants, each with their unique resistance to drought, salt – alkali, wind and sand, survive unchallenged on a land so frequently under the attack of sandstorms, and spread their seeds with the help of the desert storms, the flood and the birds even though their chances of taking root are extremely minimal.

Desert plants have their own interesting and unique survival characteristics.

In the Tarim Basin, the diversi – form leaved poplar are the tallest and mostly widely seen trees, covering an area of over 4. 5 million mu. It is an ancient specie of tree found in the desert and in salt – alkaline soil, acquiring the unique ability of growing and surviving in the most adverse of environments. From the ecological point of view, the diversi – form leaved poplar has three strange features: the shape of its leaves, its physiological functions, and its marvelous form of propagation. Young trees sprouting from the mature ones usually have leaves that are linear to minimize evaporation so that the roots can develop. Once the roots have developed and can absorb underground water, then palm – size leaves begin to grow on its crown, speeding the tree's upward growth, so that the deeper its roots, the bigger and denser its leaves, accounting for the fact that a mature tree often has leaves of three different shapes. The diversi – form leaved poplar not only has a great ability to absorb water, it is also able to expel salt and alkali from the ground on which it stands, one of the secrets why it can grow and mature on alkaline soil. The diversi – form leaved poplar also breeds in a special way, the most miraculous of which is that it takes advantage of the flood season in drought stricken areas to spread its seeds and sprout, and the maturing time of the seeds virtually coincides with the flood season. When droughts appear, it can send sprouts through its trunk or roots to propagate. According to archaeological discoveries of ancient ruins in the desert which date back over a thousand years, many ancient diversi – form leaved poplars are not yet totally dead, therefore, people have described the poplar as a tree which does not die even if it is a thousand years old, and after it is dead for a thousand years, it will still remain standing, and even after it falls down to the ground and lies there for a thousand years, it will not rot. The red willow, called the warrior of the desert because of its ability to stabilize the shifting sand, covers an area in the Tarim Basin exceeding millions of mu. After the seed of this sand – stabilizing plant takes root, it uses its body to gather the surrounding sand around itself, and after ten to twenty years of maturation, it has a very developed root system which transforms the shifting desert into sand dunes and sand hills resembling fortresses of clumps of red willow. Through the mist of the sandstorms that rage from late spring to early summer, can be seen the pink blossoms of the red willow blooming on top of each sand hill, and staying in bloom till late fall.

The desert date is also known as a sand – proof fence with its thorny body and dense branches and leaves, serving as a low forest wall that helps to counteract the onslaught of the wind and sand. In the fall, its thin – shell seeds rolls along the sandy plains looking for a chance to take root and sprout. The `poetic' bluish dogbane, with its dangling pink bell – like flowers, adds a touch of beauty to the desert edge and the shores of the Tarim River. In the late fall, when its pod – like seed pouch begins to burst, the fine woolly wings of its seeds float like the light dandelion, and after it lands, it takes advantage of the moisture of the ground to take root and waits for the coming year to grow. Because of the pliablity of its branches, it has the characteristic of bending, but not breaking in the face of a sandstorm, and so the covering of its branches exceed all other varieties of hemp, jute, flax or ramie as being the most ideal material for textile.

In the Tarim Basin, as well as the Taklimakan Desert, there are also reeds, the splendid achnatherum, and what is known as the 'desert honey' – – the camel thorns, and the cistanche salsa which has very high medicinal properties, the licorice, the Chinese ephedra, and the ground rat melon which are not only endowed with strong wind – protection and sand – stabilizing abilities, but are also of high economic value. It is exactly the growths of these desert plants of different heights and distribution that help to ward off the wind, stablize the desert, and resist soil salinization. According to statistics, there are about over 200 kinds of desert – stabilizing plants, among which over 100 kinds are shrubbery or semi – shrubbery, and the rest are perennial or annual herb in the Tarim Basin. To study the ecological laws and economic value of these desert plants, scientific research departments have set up desert research stations in the Cele Oasis at the southern edge of the Taklimakan where the desert frequently shifts, and through many years of research and experimentation, not only have great quantities of desert plants been bred and planted along the desert edge, but also valuable data collected on their wind – prevention and sand – stabilizing capacities.

胡楊林中衰退的植被
Deteriorating vegetation in a diversi – form leaved poplar forest.

頑强生長的胡楊樹
A stubbornly growing diversi – form leaved poplar tree.

沙生植物的花卉引來了彩蝶
Blossoming desert vegetation attracting butterflies.

羅布泊附近迎風而生的沙生植物
Desert plants braving the wind near the Lopnur.

塔克拉瑪干沙漠東部叢生的紅柳沙包
lusters of red – willow growing on sand dunes at the eastern s
section of the Taklimakan Desert.

干涸的枝條和紅色的新枝反映出紅柳頑强的生存本能
Tenacious survival capacities of the red willow as reflected
in the withered branches and newly grown ones.

沙漠邊緣的秋色　Autumn colors on the desert rim.

生長在重鹽碱地上的植物
Plants growing land heavily encrusted with alkali.

胡楊林生長的特殊的可食菌類
Unique, edible fungi growing in the diversi－
form leaved poplar forest.

被稱爲沙漠人參的肉叢蓉
Called 'ginseng' of the desert ——
the Cistanche salsa.

生長在荒漠中羅布麻花卉　Blossoms blooming in the waste of the Lopnur.

鋪地而生的沙生植物地老鼠瓜　Blanketing growth of 'rat' melon.

塔克拉瑪干大沙漠腹地也能見到的頑强生長的紅柳
Red willow tenaciously growing in the heart of the
Taklimakan Desert.

隨死而未倒的古胡楊樹
An erect, dead, ancient diversi – form leaved poplar tree.

塔里木東部被沙生植物圍攏的大沙山 （武　斌　攝）
A big sand hill surrounded by desert vegetation in the east of the Tarim Basin. (By Wu Bing)

胡楊是奇妙的樹種，在干旱的沙漠和戈壁中
有着神奇的吸收和寄存水份的生長特性。
The diversi – form poplar —— a unique specie with magical
capacity for absorbing and preserving water in the arid desert.

透過干涸胡楊看到的新生沙生植物依然充滿生機
Vigorously living desert vegetation amidst withered diversi – form leaved poplars.

在胡楊林中的工作的科技工作者
Scientists and technicians working in the diversi – form leaved poplar forest.

荒 漠 人 家

塔里木盆地干旱少雨，水流極缺，因而大部分地區爲戈壁所隔絕，爲沙漠所覆蓋。除了大的綠洲之外，在戈壁灘頭、沙漠深處尚有一些居住于荒漠中的人家，他們僅靠沙漠河的少許水量和地下水所潤澤的半荒漠草場繁衍生息。這些荒漠中的居民大部分都在穿越塔克拉瑪干沙漠的和田河和沙漠南端的克里雅河、亞通古斯河、安迪爾河、尼雅河以及沙漠北部、東部邊緣沿塔里木河、孔雀河一帶從事畜牧業生産。他們生活簡樸、爲人淳厚，除放牧之外，也進行一些漁獵，在與風沙干旱的搏斗中鑄就了純樸堅毅的性格。過去他們與世隔絕，今天已經同外界有了較多的接觸，尤其是來到沙漠中的旅人，成了他們最受歡迎的客人。

HOME IN THE DESERT

The Tarim Basin is arid with little precipitation, and most of it is isolated by the gobi and covered by the desert. Aside from those living in the big oases, there are families who live in the heart of the desert who depend on the little water from the desert rivers and the underground water sources that nurture the semi – barren pastures. These people raise livestock, and graze them, they have to travel across the Hotan, the Keriya, the Yatongus, the Andier, and the Niya rivers that are at the southern end of the desert, and even to the northern part of the desert and the eastern edge along the Tarim and Peacock rivers. These people lead very simple lives and are very genuine. Besides raising livestock, they also fish. In their struggles against the harsh elements of wind, sand, and drought, they have developed a very pure and simple, yet strong and unyielding nature. In the past they have been isolated from the world, but today they are beginning to have more contact with it, and tourists in the desert have become their most welcomed guests.

胡楊林里的居民在烤饢 Residents of the diversi – form leaved poplar forests baking 'nan'.

荒漠村野的秋色 Autumn colors in a desert village.

在胡楊林中放羊的牧童 Shepherd boy in the diversi – form leaved poplar forest.

沙漠南緣于田縣綠洲戴小帽的維吾爾婦女
Uygur women with miniature hats, residents
of the oasis of Yutien County on the southern
edge of the Tarim Basin.

宰羊　Slaughtering a lamb.

兒女情長　Mother and her daughter

葡萄收獲季節

依水而居 Life by the waters.

荒漠人家飲用的水井
Family well.

Bumper harvest of grapes.

就餐 Sitting down for a meal.

收獲 Harvesting.

塔里木原野上的駱駝群 Wild camels on the plains of the Tarim Basin.

沙漠中的駝夫　Leading a caravan in the desert.

塔里木河畔,原始胡楊林中的學校
A school in the primitive diversi – form leaved poplar forest in the heart of the de

和田荒漠中的牧人在風沙彌漫中,從一個綠洲走向另一個綠洲
Shepherd grazing his flock from oasis to oasis in Hotan desert, braving the sandst

和田荒漠中的老人
Senior citizen of the Hotan desert.

沙漠河克里雅的牧羊人 A Keriya shepherd by the desert river.

放牧在荒漠中的羊群
A flock of sheep foraging on the barren plains.

在沙山下虔诚做礼拜的牧人
Devout worshipers at the foot of a sand hill.

沙漠深處克里雅河畔的姑娘
Young lady by the shore of the Keriya River in the heart of the desert.

荒漠村野的秋色　Autumn colors in a desert village.

克里雅河畔的老人
An elderly citizen by the Keriya River.

沙漠人家　Desert family.

追 尋 羅 布 淖 爾 人 的 踪 迹

在塔里木盆地千余年的生態變遷中，隨着一些古老城鎮的消亡和居民的遷徙，在這片大地上留下了許多令人費解的空白。盆地東部的樓蘭便是最爲典型的一處。

一千多年前地處西域的大湖泊——羅布泊附近的樓蘭古城是史書上多有記載的絲綢之路的要冲，而公元5世紀它却在歷史文書的記載中消失了；被稱之爲爾布人，也叫羅布淖爾人的當地居民也已四處遷徙。因此這個在絲綢之路古道上曾經歷過一段繁盛時期的樓蘭古城所在地，早在公元19世紀發現以前的一段漫長時期里幾乎像月球一樣寂寞。留下的則是遍地流沙、坎坷地貌、古樹和佛寺佛塔的遺迹以及遠古墓葬，成了令人不解的秘密。樓蘭古城的消失，究其原因説法不一，有的説法是羅布泊湖址的遷移、孔雀河的斷流、土地的沙化；有的認爲是一次沙塵暴的影響；有的則認爲是戰亂。爲此，考古學家在羅布泊及其附近進行了長期而大量的考察。19世紀末、本世紀初英國人斯坦因曾在那里挖掘過古墓、考察過佛寺遺址以及被當地居民遺弃的住所。瑞典人斯文·赫定考察過羅布泊，并認定它曾是一個游移不定的湖泊，也考察了因干旱風沙所形成的特殊地貌。他的最大發現是在向導的幫助下，發現了公元前1世紀漢朝所設置的衛戍府所在的樓蘭遺址。20世紀中，中國著名考古學家黄文弼也對羅布泊地區的文化遺址、生態變遷、古代居民進行過全面考察。更值得一提的是本世紀70年代初新疆考古工作者曾在羅布泊附近發掘出一具三千多年前的少女干尸，爲此而轟動了國内外的考古界。近幾年來，許多學者文人、人種學家和旅游探險的人爲了追尋羅布人的踪迹，他們終于在塔里木盆地東北邊緣乃至和田地區的洛甫綠洲發現了羅布人的后裔，通過對一些百歲老人的訪問，追述了羅布人的歷史和傳説。據講，他們的祖先曾在羅布泊一帶從事畜牧和漁獵，由于孔雀河的注入，充沛的湖水和良好的植被曾經是非常富庶的地方，他們的飲食結構，除肉食和獲取的獵物，主要以食魚爲主，或炖煮，或用紅柳條穿上，燒烤全魚，撒上蒲黄，味道十分鮮美。由于湖泊周圍蘆葦叢生，他們也嚼白嫩的蘆根，也喝玉米面摻沙棗的糊糊。大都身體强壯，百歲老人也多。從他們祖先由羅布泊附近最后留住的羅布莊、阿不旦莊算起也已有很多年代了。今天的羅布人后裔約有1.3萬人，他們大部分是操羅布方言的維吾爾人。他們最大的變化是由過去生活在孔雀河下游的羅布泊地區，改爲生活在塔里木河下游半荒漠草場和胡楊林中，從事畜牧和漁業生産，也種植一些瓜果和農作物。他們的傳統習俗雖然已經淡化，但仍保留了一些祖先的習性，如用挖空樹心制作名爲"卡盆"的魚船，湖邊的烤魚等。他們用古老羅布淖爾民歌演唱的美麗傳説描述的日常生活勞作的情景，也都充滿了古老的格調，十分動聽。當地政府已經決定選一處胡楊林區建一個羅布人村落，衣食住行、歌舞漁獵、誦經禮拜全部模仿羅布人的生活原貌，讓這古老民族的習俗再現于人們的面前。

現今生活在若羌綠洲的羅布人家
Lopnurian presently living in the
Rouqiang oasis.

生活在孔雀河下游羅布人的后裔依然保留着喜歡食魚的習慣
Descendants of the Lopnurian living at the lower reaches of the Peacock River retain their habitual love for fish in their diet.

孔雀河下游從事放牧的羅布老人
Elderly Lopnurian shepherd grazing his flock at the lower reaches of the Peacock River.

LOOKING FOR TRACES OF THE LOPNURIANS

With the ecological changes that have taken place in the Tarim Basin in the last millennium and more, and with the disappearance of ancient cities and towns and the migration of their residents, many blanks have been left on this land that puzzle the world. The most typical of which is Loulan.

The ancient city of Loulan which had so often appeared in historical annals and which had been a junction of the ancient Silk Road, was located near Lopnur – – a big lake in the Western Territory, disappeared from historical records at around 5th century A. D., and its residents, the Lopnurians, had migrated to the four corners. Therefore, what had been a thriving city on the ancient Silk Road lapsed into oblivion until its discovery in the 19th century. What it had left behind was a shifting desert, a rugged landform, ancient trees, ruins of Buddhist temples and burial grounds of forgotten times, and became an unsolved puzzle. There seems to have been more than one explanation for the disappearance of Loulan. Some say it was due to the change in the lake location and the drying up of the Peacock River which resulted in the desertification of the land; others think it was buried by a giant sandstorm, and still others think it was destroyed by war. To find the answers, archaeologists have undertaken long – term and large – scale studies of the areas in the vicinity of the Lopnur. In the late 19th and early 20th century, the Britisher, Aurel Stein had excavated ancient tombs and surveyed ruins of Buddhist temples, and houses abandoned by local residents. The Swede, Sven Hedin, had also surveyed the Lopnur, and he recognized it to be a lake that had shifted position, he also surveyed the unique land features formed by the arid wind and sand. His greatest find was made with the help of his guide when he discovered the garrison established by the Han Dynasty in 1 century B. C. at the Loulan ruins. In the 20th century, the famed Chinese archaeologist, Huang Wenbi, had made a comprehensive study of the Lopnur, which included its cultural ruins, ecological change, and ancient residents. Worth mentioning is the discovery by the Xinjiang archaeologists of the dried corpse of a young girl who lived over 1, 300 years ago that rocked archaeological circles around the world. In recent years, many scholars,

ethnologists, explorers and tourists have come to look for traces of the Lopnurians, and they eventually found their descendents living in the northeastern edge of the Tarim and even in the Lopu oasis of the Hotan Prefecture. In interviews with some of the centenarians, they recounted the history and legends of the Lopnurians. According to them, their ancestors had once lived in the Lopnur area had raised livestock and fished. The area had been richly covered with vegetation due to the abundance of water from the Peacock River. Their diet structure, besides meat and game, was mainly fish, whether stewed or skewered on willow twigs and barbecued whole, and sprinkled with a spice, was very palatable. Because the surrounding areas of the lake were thickly grown with reeds, they often chewed their white, tender roots, or ate gruel made from cornflour mixed with fruit of the narrow – leave oleaster. The people were big and strong and many of them lived to be over a hundred years old. It has been many generations since their ancestors lived in the Lopnur and Abudan days. Their descendents now number 13, 000 and most of them are Uygur who speak the Lopuur dialect. Their biggest change is moving from their former residence at the lower reaches of the Peacock River in the Lopnur area to the semi – barren plains and diversi – form leaved poplar forests at the lower reaches of the Tarim River to continue raising their livestock and fish, and also growing melons, fruit and agricultural crops. They have forsaken some of their traditional customs, but still retain some habits left over from their ancestors, such as hollowing trees to make the "kapan" fishing boat, barbecuing fish by the lakeside, and others. They use the ancient forms of Lopnurian folksongs and beautiful legends to describe their daily life and labor which are full of ancient airs and most pleasant to the ears. The local government has decided to designate an area in a diversi – form leaved poplar forest as a Lopnurian village where dress, food, housing, lifestyle, song and dance, fishing and hunting, and even worship are entirely simulated from the original lifestyle of the Lopnurians, so that present – day people can see for themselves the customs and habits of this ancient people.

在湖畔，今天的維吾爾人依然保留用"卡盆"漁船捕魚和在岸邊烤魚的習慣
Present day Uygur living by the lake still retain their habits of fishing in "kapan" boats and barbecuing their catch by the shore.

羅布人的村頭，豎立起標識，便于路人尋訪
A flying standard at a Lopnurian village for visitors to identify.

古老壁畫的藝術長廊

石窟寺是絲綢之路重要的佛教文化遺迹。它環繞塔里木盆地乃至吐魯番盆地構成了許多處的壁畫藝術長廊。沿着整個絲綢之路的走向，一直綿延至敦煌、河西走廊、隴海路沿綫，特別是塔里木盆地的石窟寺，就目前留存下來的不下二三十處。如果包括盆地南緣被流沙湮没和因其他原因被徹底毁損的繪有壁畫的寺廟群就更多了。今天保存比較完好的大部分分布于盆地北部沿天山南坡和吐魯番盆地的石窟寺，其中最爲著名的要屬位于拜城縣的克孜爾石窟寺，位于庫車的庫木吐拉、克孜爾尕哈、森姆賽木，位于焉耆的明屋和位于吐魯番盆地的伯孜克里克

等千佛洞。新疆的壁畫藝術是隨絲綢之路的興起，在佛教由西向東傳入的過程中形成的。后來汲取了希臘和中原文化而顯現着豐富的文化内涵和絢麗的色彩。約建于公元 3—5 世紀的克孜爾、庫木吐拉、伯孜克里克千佛洞自魏晋至宋元延續千年，反映不同歷史時期的壁畫現已整理編號的就有四百多個洞窟。它們記録了絲綢之路重要的歷史篇章，給后人留下了不可磨滅的文化藝術寶藏。成爲今天人們研究歷史的重要遺址。

AN 'ART GALLERY' OF ANCIENT MURALS

Grottoes are important ruins of Buddhist culture of the Silk Road. They add up to make an art gallery of murals that surround the Tarim Basin and even the Turpan Basin. There are at least twenty to thirty such art galleries along the Silk Road, especially the cave temples of the Tarim Basin, extending all the way to Dunhuang, the Hexi Corridor, and along the Longhai Railroad. That number is greater if we include the caves that have been buried by sand at the southern edge of the Basin, and murals in the clusters of temples and monasteries which have been, for one reason or another, completely destroyed. Presently, the relatively well-protected ones are mainly distributed along the north of the Basin along the southern slope of the Tianshan Mountains and the grottoes in the Turpan Basin, of which the best known are the Kizil Caves in Baicheng County, the Kumtola, the Kizilgahar, and the Simsem in Kuqa, the Mingoi in Yanji, and the Bezkilik in Turpan. The mural art of Xinjiang began with the Silk Road, during the eastward dissemination of Buddhism from the West. It later also absorbed the best of the Greek culture and the Central Plains culture to attain its colorful and rich cultural content. The building of the Kizil, Kumtola, and Bezkilik caves began around the 3rd to 5th century A. D. and continued for a thousand years through the Wei – Jin Dynasties to the Yuan – Song Dynasties, with murals in over 400 caves that reflect the different historical times. They not only recorded the important historical pages of the Silk Road, but also left for posterity a trove of cultural art that cannot be obliterated. They have become important ruins for people to study history.

克孜爾千佛洞是絲綢古道上的著名石窟寺,它早於敦煌一百多年
The renowned Kizil Thousand Buddha Grottoes of the ancient Silk Road are 100 years older than those of Dunhuang.

克孜爾千佛洞,迎來了國内外衆多客人的參觀考察
The restored facade of the Kizil Grottoes being visited by foreign and domestic tourists.

克孜千佛洞中獨特的菱形壁畫
Unique diamond – shaped murals of the Kizil Grottoes.

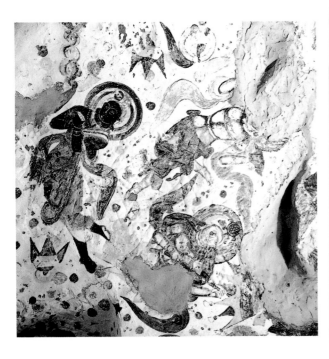

在克孜爾石窟樹起佛經翻譯家鳩摩羅什的銅像
A bronze statue of Jumorosh, the translator of sutras, in the Kizil Grottoes.

克孜爾千佛洞 38 窟壁畫　Murals in the No. 38 grotto of Kizil.

克孜爾千佛洞窟頂的飛天　Apsaras on the ceilings of the Kizil Grottoes.

克孜爾千佛洞的壁畫
Murals in the Kizil Grottoes.

克孜爾千佛洞中王子出海圖壁畫
Mural of the 'Prince emerging from the sea' in the
Kizil Grottoes.

克孜爾千佛洞的壁畫
Murals in the Kizil Grottoes.

森木塞姆千佛洞外景　　Exterior view of the Simsem Thousand Buddha Caves.

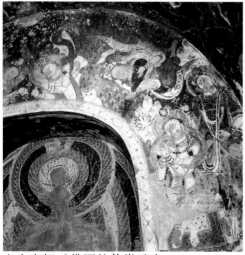

森木塞姆千佛洞的伎樂壁畫
Murals of musicians in the Simsem Caves.

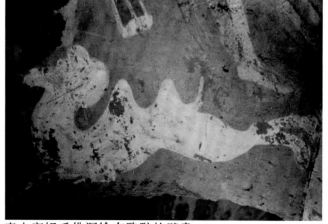

森木塞姆千佛洞繪有駱駝的壁畫
Murals of camels in the Simsem Caves.

庫木吐拉千佛洞46窟壁畫
Mural in No. 46 cave of Kumtola.

庫木吐拉千佛洞外景　Exterior view of the Kumtola Thousand Buddha Caves.

庫木吐拉千佛洞新 2 號窟壁畫　Mural in New No. 2 cave of Kumtola.

伊斯蘭文化

公元 10 世紀，伊斯蘭教最先傳入塔里木盆地，到 13 世紀后波及天山南北。因此，伊斯蘭文化在新疆歷史發展過程中有着重要的影響。除了建築藝術，在文學藝術方面，著名的《突厥語大詞典》和文學巨著《福樂智慧》以及音樂史詩十二木卡姆等都出自當時的喀什古城和葉爾羌汗國。這些著作和詩歌、音樂篇章已被翻譯成多種文字，成爲中華民族乃至世界文化的遺產。上述歷史人物穆罕默德·喀什噶里、玉素甫·哈斯·哈吉甫、阿曼尼沙汗的墓地都已在原有的遺址上修葺一新，成爲人們瞻仰的勝地。而古老的建築，如著名的艾提尕爾清真寺、阿帕霍加墓、莎車縣的加曼清真寺、庫車大寺等等，都已成爲重要的文化遺址。伊斯蘭建築藝術風格對當今的建築業也産生着重要的影響。

ISLAMIC CULTURE

Islam first entered the Tarim Basin in 10th century A. D., and by 13th century A. D. it had spread to the north and south of the Tianshan Mountains. Therefore, Islamic culture has had an important influence in the historical development of Xinjiang. In addition to architectural art, its influence was also felt in cultural arts; the masterpiece of "The Turkic Lexicon" and the literal work of "Kutad Kubelig" as well as the musical epic of "The Twelve Mukkam" all appeared at the time of ancient Kashgar and the Yerqiang Khanate. These masterpeices have been translated into different languages and have become a part of the cultural heritage of not only China, but also of the world. The tombs of the historical figures – – Makmut Kashgarri, Yusuf Haas Hajji, and Amanisahan – – authors of the afore – mentioned works, have all been renovated and become places for people to come and pay their respects. Ancient architecture, such as the Id Kah Mosque of Kashgar, the Apakhoja Mausoleum, the Gaman Mosque of Shache, and the Great Mosque of Kuqa have all become key cultural ruins. The style of Islamic architectural art still wields a strong influence in present – day architecture.

喀什清真寺建築　Architecture of Kashgar Mosque.

伊斯蘭墓葬群 Islamic tombs.

陵墓內景 Interior of the mausoleum.

福樂智慧作者玉素甫哈斯・阿吉甫陵墓大門

Gateway to the mausoleum of Yusuf Haas Hajji, author of "*Kutad Kubelig.*"

阿帕克霍加墓旁古老清真寺廊柱
Corridor columns of ancient mosque beside the Apakhoja Mausoleum.

伊斯蘭墓葬群 Islamic tombs.

位于塔里木北部著名的庫車清真大寺　　The famous Kuqa Great Mosque at the north of the Tarim Basin.

庫車著名的伊斯蘭傳教士遺址
Famous ruins of Islamic mission of Kuqa.

庫車大清真寺内景
Interior view of the Kuqa Great Mosque.

突厥語大辭典的作者穆罕默德·喀什噶里的陵墓
Mausoleum of Makmut Kashggari, author of "*The Turkic Lexicon.*"

陵墓内景
Interior of the mausoleum.

福樂智慧作者玉素甫哈斯·阿吉甫陵墓大門
Gateway to the mausoleum of Yusuf Haas Hajji, author of "*Kutad Kubelig.*"

喀什古地城著名的伊斯蘭古建築阿帕克霍加墓(又稱香妃墓)
The Apakhoja Masusoleum, famous ancient Islamic architecture of Kashgar.

墓室門的雕飾之一
Engraved gates to the tombs (1).

伊斯蘭古建築雕飾之二
Engraved ornamentations of ancient Islamic
architecture(2).

阿帕克霍加墓旁古老清真寺廊柱
Corridor columns of ancient mosque beside the Apakhoja Mausoleum.

莎車加曼清真寺外景
Exterior view of the Gaman Mosque in Shache.

莎車加曼清真寺內景
Interior view of the Gaman Mosque of Shache.

十二木卡姆作者阿曼尼莎汗的陵墓
Mausoleum of Amanisahan, authoress of *The Twelve Mukkam.*"

莎車縣伊斯蘭復古建築
Revival of ancient Islamic architecture in Shache County.

喀什維吾爾居民庭院之一　A Uygur family courtyard in Kashgar(1).

喀什維吾爾居民庭院之三
A Uygur family courtyard in Kashgar(3).

喀什維吾爾居民庭院之二
A Uygyr family courtyard in Kashgar(2).

古城喀什的小巷
A small alleyway in old town Kashgar.

喀什市小巷中的過街居民住宅 （武 斌 攝）
Arcaded residence in an alley in Kashgar.　　(By Wu Bing)

伊斯蘭建築中的瓷碟花飾
Floral plate designs in Islamic architecture.

在古爾邦節中喀什艾提尕的廣場景象
A view of festivities on the square in front of the Id Kah Mosque in Kashgar.

艾提尕爾清真寺禮拜堂中的穹頂
Domed ceiling in the worship hall of the Id Kah Mosque.

艾提尕爾清真寺内部裝飾　Interior decorations of the Id Kah Mosque.

艾提尕爾清真寺及其廣場上的鐘樓
The Id Kah Mosque and its Bell Tower on the square.

葉爾羌河兩岸的沃野
Fertile plains on the shores of the Yerqiang River.

绿洲經濟　綠洲居民

　　塔里木盆地干旱少雨，水流極缺，因此人們的經濟活動區域爲戈壁沙漠所隔，形成了綠洲經濟的特色。整個盆地的綠洲大部分分布于塔克拉瑪干沙漠的周圍，個別小的荒漠綠洲則隨着沙漠河深入到塔克拉瑪干的腹地。塔里木盆地綠洲沃野面積大小不一，它們都是以 10—2500 平方公里不等的綠洲面積出現在整個盆地。沃野總面積爲 14600 平方公里，約占盆地面積的六十分之一。這些綠洲與其臨近山的高度和雪源的多寡有極密切的關系。如位于帕米爾高原下，喀什河、克孜爾河流經的疏勒綠洲面積爲 2650 平方公里，葉爾羌河流經的莎車綠洲爲 2600 平方公里，而阿克蘇河、和田河所流經的阿克蘇綠洲、和田綠洲，面積都很大。而在山勢比較低的東部盆地氣候干燥，水源不足，因此綠洲沃野分布也較小，像若羌綠洲面積僅 30 平方公里。塔里木盆地的綠洲居民大部分爲維吾爾族，也有一部分漢、回及柯爾克孜、烏孜別克、塔吉克等民族。在長期的歷史發展過程中，綠洲居民以從事農業、畜牧業生產爲主，但由于綠洲沃野面積的大小和手工業經濟的發展程度不同，在一些大的綠洲中便形成了一些由著名城鎮構成的經濟活動的中心區域。如喀什綠洲的喀什噶爾古城，和田綠洲的和田市、葉爾羌沃野的莎車，塔里木河沿岸的阿克蘇、庫車、庫爾勒等。這些城鎮手工業和商業都很發達，以當地人稱之爲"巴扎"(集日) 形式的經濟交往活動十分頻繁，僅喀什

每當"巴扎"天來自郊野的農民達到二十多萬人，集市上農副產品在此集散，各種商品琳琅滿目，尤其是手工業產品豐富多彩。在長期的歷史發展過程中，這些綠洲也形成了各自的特色，從維吾爾人喜愛的花帽到工藝小刀；從艾特萊斯綢到各種花色的氈毯，形狀各異的陶器，不僅地方風格濃郁，也表現出綠洲居民年深日久精湛的工藝水平。

　　在以養殖蠶桑、出產絲綢而著名的和田綠洲，繅絲織毯業已有千余年的歷史。特別是毛織物，從被沙漠湮没約一千多年的尼雅、樓蘭遺址中出土的各色花飾的毛氈、地毯和毛織品，到近期和田綠洲山普拉古墓葬中出土的公元 1 世紀左右的毛織彩帶、男女毛織衣褲，無一件不是織造精細，色彩艷麗的毛織精品。

　　塔里木盆地有着瓜果之鄉的美稱，在園藝生產中，由于早晚溫差大，光照時間長，瓜果不僅香甜，品種也很多。出產于喀什綠洲的石榴、薄皮桃李和葡萄，庫車盛產的小白杏，阿圖什的無花果，和田的石榴、核桃等都是水果中的佳品，不僅可以鮮吃而且晾制出的干果糖分也很高。

　　今天，隨着對外開放的不斷擴大，交通信息的暢通和幾處口岸的開放，塔里木綠洲已經結束了與外界的隔絕，出現了新的經濟振興的勢頭。

鳥瞰和田的戈壁綠洲

A bird's – eye view of the oases in the desert of Hotan.

OASIS ECONOMY, OASIS PEOPLE

The Tarim Basin is dry with little precipitation and serious lack of water, therefore, the areas for people's economic activities are isolated by the gobi desert, forming a unique oasis economy. Most of the oases of the entire basin are distributed along the periphery of the Taklimakan Desert, and individual smaller ones are even located in the interior of the desert following the flow of the desert rivers. Fertile oases of the Tarim Basin vary in size, ranging from 10 – 2, 500 square kilometers. The oases cover 14, 600 square kilometers, making up for one – sixtieth of the basin area. These oases are closely related to the altitude of the nearby mountains and difference in snowmelt. Take for example the Shule Oasis, measuring 2, 650 square kilometers, which is located below the Pamir Plateau along where the Kash and Kizil rivers run, and the Shache Oasis, measuring 2, 600 square kilometers, along which the Yerqiang river runs, whereas the Aksu Oasis and the Hotan Oasis which are located along where the Aksu and Hotan rivers run, cover bigger areas. In the east of the basin where the mountains are of relatively lower elevation and the climate is arid with insufficient water, the oases there are scattered and small, such as the Rouqiang Oasis which covers a mere 30 square kilometers. The majority of the people in the Tarim oases are Uygur, with some Han, Hui, Kirgiz, Uzbek and Tajik peoples. In the process of historical development, the oasis people mainly engage in agriculture and animal husbandry, while the development of the economy of the handicraft industry is related to the size of the oasis. In some big oases there have emerged famous townships which have become centers of the handicraft industry and other commercial activities, such as the ancient city of Kashgar of the Kashgar Oasis, the city of Hotan of the Hotan Oasis, Shache of the Yerqiang Oasis, and Aksu, Kuqa, and Korle which are along the shores of the Tarim River. These cities and townships have a very developed handicraft industry and commerce as can be witnessed by what the local people call `the bazaar', where economic activities thrive. In Kashgar alone, each `bazaar' day at least over 200, 000 farmers from the nearby countryside flock to the market where agricultural byproducts and centered and distributed, and where there is an enormous variety of colorful commodities, especially all kinds of handcrafted products. In the process of development, the oases have all form their own unique characteristics in handicrafts, from the embroidered caps that the Uygur people love to the artistic knives, from the atlas silks to the vast variety of carpets, and pottery of different shapes and sizes which are not only unique in their exotic features, but also reflect the long – standing, excellent craftsmanship of the oasis people.

The Hotan Oasis, long known for its sericulture and silk production, has had a history of over 1, 000 years in its silk reeling and carpet weaving industry, especially in its woolen textile as can be proven by archaeological finds of woolen blankets, carpets, and fabric unearthed from the ruins of Niya and Loulan which had been buried under the desert for over a millennium, to the recent excavations in the ancient tombs of Shanpula in the Hotan Oasis which date back to the 1st century A. D., uncovering woolen woven colored belts, man's and woman's sweaters and pants, all of which were choice woolen items finely woven and beautifully and colorfully designed.

The Tarim Basin has the complimentary name of "Home of the Fruit and Melon." In horticultural products, because of its great difference in day and night temperatures and long sunlight hours, its fruit and melon are not only fragrant and sweet, but they also come in a great variety. The pomegranate of the Kashgar Oasis, its thin – skin peaches, plums and grapes, the white apricots of Kuqa, the figs of Artux, and the pomegranates and walnuts of Hotan are all choice varieties of fruits which are not only delectable eaten fresh, but their sugar content is especially high when dried.

Presently, with the penetration of the development, the unimpeded flow of traffic, communication and information, and the opening up of seveal land ports, the Tarim Oasis has ended her days of being isolated from the world, and is now ready to face the challenges of an economic rejuvenation.

在塔克拉瑪干沙漠西緣栽種的防風林帶
A windbreak forest belt on the western edge of the Taklimakan Desert.

玉龍喀什河的引水工程
A diversion works project of the Ulungur – Kash River.

在和田綠洲中約800年的古核桃樹
An 800 – year old walnut tree in an oasis of Hotan.

塔里木墾荒地上的收獲 Harvesting on the reclaimed land of the Tarim.

塔里木河下游的大西海子水庫呈現出漁歌唱晚的景色〈武斌 攝〉
Evening song —— Fishermen returning with their catch at the Daxihaizi Reservoir at the lower reaches of the Tarim River. (By Wu Bing)

沙漠湖泊人歡魚躍 Happy people and leaping fish on a desert lake.

農墾團場飼養的鹿群 Deer raised on a land reclamation farm.

集市上的售帽人
A hat maker selling his ware in the market.

古色古香的民間地毯
Hand – woven carpets with antique and quaint designs.

喀什集市上的店鋪
Shops in the Kashgar Bazaar.

喀什綠洲歡聚的人們　Happy people of the Kashgar oasis.

熱情好客的綠洲居民　Hospitable and warm people of the oasis.

老人和孩子
The elderly and the very young.

和田綠洲居民在制作地毯　Residents of the Hotan Oasis weaving carpets

織毯姑娘 Young carpet – weaver.

織毯老人 Master carpet – weaver.

各式花色的和田地毯遠銷國內外
Colorful Hotan carpets exported to four corners of the earth.

艾 特 萊 斯 綢

　　艾特萊斯綢,是維吾爾、烏孜別克婦女喜用的一種圖案別致的傳統衣料,內地稱之爲和田綢。老年婦女喜穿黑白花的,以顯得樸素、莊重、大方、老成;姑娘們喜穿紅綠彩花的,以顯得華麗、活潑、富有青春感。

　　艾特萊斯綢的織造方法與內地傳統的提花織法不同,它在織前先按紋樣及色彩扎染經綫,再經藝人憑記憶在拉經時排列就序,織后緯綫完全藏于經底。這種織法關內實爲罕見。

Altas Silk

Atlas is a kind of silk fabric with intricate and unique patterns that Uygur and Uzbek women like to use for their dresses. It is called Hotan silk by the hinterland people. The older women like to wear dresses made of Atlas with black – white designs and patterns, while young women and girls like the multi – colored variety. The older women in Atlas with black – white patterns look dignified and elegant, while the young women and girls in colorful Atlas look resplendent and brimming with youthful vigour.

The weaving of Altas is different from that of the traditional weaving used in the hinterland. First, the craftsmen have the silk yarn(warp) dyed according to the planned pattern they intend to weave, and then mount it on the 100m according to the patterns and designs and then weave from memory. In the weaving of Atlas, the weft yarn is completely hidden beneath the warp. This process of weaving is rarely found in the hinterland of China.

和田綠洲居民有着古老的養蠶繅絲的傳統
Ancient tradition of Hotan people —— raising silkworms.

穿着艾特萊斯綢的維吾爾族少女在集市上出售她紡織的土綢
Girls dressed in colorful Atlas silks they have woven and promoting their own handicraft.

色彩的艾特莱斯綢 Colorful Atlas

古老的繅絲工藝
The ancient craft of silk reeling.

集市上的工藝小刀及其制作 The handcrafting process and finished product of knives in the market.

英 吉 沙 小 刀

英吉沙小刀是維吾爾族的傳統手工藝品，造型別致，制作精巧，既可作刀具，又有藝術欣賞價值，是頗具特色的絲綢之路旅游紀念品。

英吉沙小刀多數爲彎刀，刀把有木質的、角質的、銅質的、銀質的，非常講究。無論哪一種刀把，英吉沙的工匠們都要在上面鑲嵌上色彩鮮明的圖案花紋，有的甚至用寶石來點綴，玲瓏華貴，令人愛不釋手。除英吉沙小刀外，庫車的"孔雀刀"也已遠近聞名。

少數民族男子都有佩帶小刀的習俗，身邊能有一把華麗別致的小刀，便增添一種風度。

The Yengisar Dagger

Yengisar daggers ane ingeniously handcrafted. They are the famous traditional handcrafts of the Uygur people. The daggers ane of unique designs and exquisite workmanship. They not only serve as knives, but alsoas ornaments, highly appreciated by local and foreign tourists as souvenir of the "Silk Road."

Most Yengisar daggers have curved blades, and hilts made of either wood, horn , copper or silk , and inlaid with fine designs and patterns of bright colors, and some are enen inlaid with gems, making the daggers a work of art that is highly valued. Besides the Yengisar daggers, the Kuqa" Peacook Dagger"is also well known near and far . The local men are accostomed to wearing daggers. A man will look quite impressive wearing a beatifully made yengisar dagger.

喀什綠洲中土陶生産歴史悠久 Pottery with ancient history in the Kashgar oasis.

喀什噶爾的民族手工藝品蜚聲中外，深受新疆各族人民喜愛。色彩絢麗的小花帽、民族樂器、英吉沙小刀以及地毯、首飾等馳名産品，遠銷全疆各地和内地，其中有的已打入國際市場。

The handicrafts of Kashgar have a distinctive Uygur style. They have earned international fame and a ready market among various ethnic peoples of Xingjiang. For instance, embroidered hats with patterns of bright colours, ethnic musical instruments, Yengisar knives, carpets and ornaments are brandname goods enjoying an enthusiartic market all over Xingjiang as well as in other places If China. Some of them have won their share of acknowledgment on the international market.

異彩紛呈的各式花帽是綠洲集市上最受歡迎的工藝品　　The most welcome items on the market —— beautifully embroidered caps.

乘車來逛巴扎的綠洲居民 Oasis residents riding to the market.

富有維吾爾風格的樂器多種多樣
Various musical instruments of strong
ethnic Uygur features.

在巴扎上的停車場 A parking lot in the bazaar.

制作民族首飾的攤販
Smiths handcrafting ethnic jewelry.

富有特色的鑲嵌木箱 Uniquely embossed trunks.

出售手工製品的工匠 Smiths selling their hand – crafted products.

集市一角
A corner of the market.

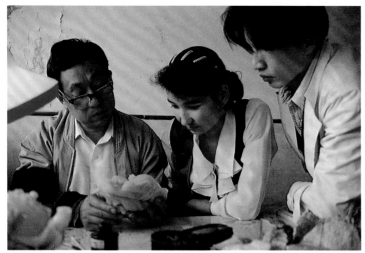

传授玉雕技艺　Passing on the handicraft of jade carving.

玉雕产品 Products of carved jade.

和田集市上出售的天然玉石　Natural jade sold on the Hotan market.

和田河上的采玉人　Looking for jade in the Hotan River.

馳名中外的庫爾勒香梨
World – renowned fragrant pears of Korle.

塔里木的特産木瓜
The quince —— a Tarim specialty.

　　塔里木的瓜果品種多，質量好，而且有許多現在已經十分難見。杏、桃、李、梨、葡萄、石榴、無花果、巴旦木、櫻桃、阿月渾子、伽師瓜和西瓜都是上品。其中葉城的石榴、蟠桃，喀什的無花果、櫻桃，英吉沙的巴旦木，伽師和麥蓋提的甜瓜更是譽滿全疆，行銷中外，質量之佳，令人贊嘆。

　　Kashi's melons and fruits are well known for thier high quality and the number of rare varieties. The high quality is seen in the apricot, peach, plum, pear, grape, pomegranate, fig , badnmo, cherry, ayuehunzi, Jiashimelon and water – melon. Those with special fame in Xingjiang include: The pomegranate and flat peach from Yecheng , fig and cherry from Kashi and badanmo and Jiashi melon from Yengisar, and sweet melon from Markit. They enjoy a ready market both in China and abroad with their superb quality.

塔里木緑洲盛産各種水果
Various kinds of fruit produced in the Tarim oases.

塔里木南縁優質的無花果
Quality figs from the southern edge of the Tarim Basin.

塔里木緑洲也盛産着優質的葡萄
Choice grapes abundantly produced in the Tarim oases.

各種干果 Various kinds of dried fruit.

馳名的伽師瓜 The famous melons of Jiashi.

沿塔里木四周都盛産各種品種的杏
A variety of apricots grown in areas surrounding the Tarim Basin.

著名的喀什葉城石榴
The well-known promegranates of Yecheng, Kashgar.

各種甘甜的葡萄　A multiple variety of grapes.

石油、棉花———一黑一白資源的開發

在新疆的經濟發展中，開發以石油、棉花爲主體的一黑一白資源已成爲經濟結構的重要部分，而塔里木盆地則是建設開發上述兩種資源的主要地區。

從地圖上看，塔里木盆地是中國最大的沉積盆地。資料表明它也是世界上僅存的少數幾個尚未進行油氣勘探的大型沉積盆地之一。正是基于這種認識，從 50 年代開始，特別是 70 年代以來，中國的石油工作者以塔克拉瑪干爲舞臺，通過中外合作和技術引進，在塔里木盆地周圍和盆地腹部的沙海進行了大量的地震勘測。近年來，又在其北部及腹心地帶建起了飛機場，竪起井架開始了鑽探。目前塔里木盆地的石油勘探，已從區域概查轉入油瀝地帶普查。經過中國石油天然氣總公司和原地質礦產部的共同努力，通過鑽探已經證實，塔里木盆地北、西、南的石油探井都有油氣顯示。特別是通過近兩年的勘探開發，主要工作的五個區域，即大漠北部邊緣的輪臺縣以南地區、東河塘地區、英買力地區、大沙漠腹地的塔中地區以及 1990 年開始勘探的吉拉克地區，都打出了高產油氣流，找到了大型、特大型整裝油氣田，並且已經開始形成年產 500 萬噸原油的產能。最近，經過塔里木石油勘探指揮部的努力，又在沙漠西部探明了又一個沙漠油氣田。在勘探開發中他們還通過招標引來國際上的幾個大石油公司共同參與塔里木的石油勘探開發。通過石油勘探也發現塔克拉瑪干沙海之下有着豐富的水資源，他們在 22 萬平方公里的流沙區打出了 76 個人工出水點，水將會給塔克拉瑪干的開發帶來新生機，也改變了人們過去對這里滴水全無的看法。除了石油和水資源，塔克拉瑪干地下還埋藏有銅、鐵、金、鎢、鉻、錳，蘊藏着超過千萬噸的鹽硝和石膏。塔里木已經成了人們心目中的石油之海、希望之海。

塔里木盆地是中國農業資源的寶地，人工灌溉、早晚溫差大、光照時間長的生態環境，形成特殊的農作物和畜牧品種的優良品質。爲了進一步開發農業資源，新疆維吾爾自治區人民政府在全區的經濟發展中把發展棉花生產擺在了重要位置，尤其是塔里木爲形成一黑一白重點資源的發展，普遍擴大了棉花種植面積，加大了技術含量，使棉花生產連年增產，出現了百萬擔皮棉縣和幾個平均畝產雙百斤皮棉縣，總產量比 90 年代之前有了成倍增長，由于優越的生態環境，棉花不僅產量高，而且纖維長、質地白。在塔里木河中段的阿克蘇和庫爾勒，新疆生產建設兵團團場還建起了長絨棉生產基地。隨着改革開放的不斷深化，除棉花之外，各種糧食作物，以三北羊和半粗毛羊爲主體的畜牧業，以及林業、瓜果蔬菜等都獲得了連年的豐收。塔里木一黑一白資源的開發定會給新疆經濟帶來更大的繁榮。

在塔克拉瑪干沙漠中勘探
Prospecting in the heart of the Taklimakan Desert.

沙漠機場　An airport in the desert.

PETROLEUM AND COTTON
DEVELOPING THE BLACK AND WHITE RESOURCES

In the development of Xinjiang, an important part of its economic structure is the development of petroleum and cotton--its blac kandwhite resources, and the Tarim Basin is where these two resources originate.

From the map, we can see that the Tarim Basin is China's largest sedimentary basin. Data has proven that it is the few remaining largesedimentary basins in the world which have not yet been explored for oil and gas. It is precisely based on this finding that beginning in the '50s, especially in the' 70s, that Chinese petroleum workers have used the Taklimakan a stage, through Sino-foreign cooperation and introduction of technology, large scale seismic surveys have been done in the deserts in the interior and surrounding areas of the Tarim Basin. In recent years, airports have been builtin its northand its interior, and oil rigs have started their drillings. At present, petroleum exploration in the Tarim has progressed from regional general prospecting to oil-pitch belt surveying. Under the joint efforts of the Head Office of the China Petroleum and Natural Gas Company and the former Ministry of Geological Mineral Products, it has been verified through drilling that oil wells in the north, west, and southern section of the Tarim Basin contain oil and gas. Especially through the development and survey of the two recent years, the five main working areas, i. e. the southern region, the eastern river region, the Yingmaili region of Luntai County at the northern rim of the desert, and the Tarim central region in the heart of the desert and the Jerak region which was saw initial prospecting in 1990. All of them have produced high-yielding oil and gas flows, and large and super-large complete oil and gas fields have been found, and capacity for an annual production of 500 tons of crude oil is already in formation. Most recently, another desert oil/gas field was discovered in the western part of the desert through the efforts of the Tarim Petroleum Survey Headquarters. In the process of survey and development, the TPSH has had several international major oil companies join its efforts through bidding. In their explorations they have also discovered that there are rich water resources under the desert sand, and have drilled 76 water-sprouting holes in a shifting desert zone of 220, 000 square kilometers which will bring new life to the development of the desert, and change the long, ill-conceived fact that not a drop of water was to be found in the desert. Besides the resources of oil and water under the desert, the Tarim is also rich in deposits of copper, iron, gold, tungsten, chromium, manganese, and dozen million tons of saltpetre and gypsum. The Tarim has already become the 'Petroleum Sea', as well as the 'Sea of Hope' in the eyes of the people.

The Tarim Basin is also a treasure trove of China's agricultural resources. Its artificially irrigated fields, its ecological environment of huge temperature difference within the 24-hour day, and its long sunlight hours have all contributed to form the unique quality species of crops and breeds of livestock. To further develop its agricultural resources, the People's Government of the Xinjiang Uygur Autonomous Region has placed cotton production in an important position in the development of its economy. In the quest of building the Tarim Basin into a base for the 'black' and 'white' key resources, there has been a general increase in cotton-growing acreage and technology content in its production which resulted in consecutive increased yields. Many cotton-producing counties are now known as 'million-dan ginned cotton counties', or counties with average per mu yield of 100 kilograms of ginned cotton. Gross production has grown by leaps and bounds since the '90s, and thanks to the favorable ecological environment, the cotton yield is not only high, but its quality is also superb, long-stapled and white. The Xinjiang Production and Construction Corps has built a long-staple cotton production base in Aksu and Korle which are located in the mid-section of the Tarim River. With the deepening of the reform and opening up, besides growing cotton and other grain crops, animal husbandry such as the breeding of the Sanbei sheep and the semi-coarse wool sheep in the main, forestry, fruit, melon and produce have all had consecutive bumper harvests. The development of the 'black' and 'white' resources of the Tarim is sure to bring greater prosperity to the economy of Xinjiang.

為鑽井隊開路 Blazing the trail for the oil drilling teams.

柯克亞油氣流
Flow of gas and oil from Kokya.

塔中一井出油景觀　View of oil spouting from Well No. 1 of the Tarim Oil Fields.

沙漠變通途
The desert has become a thoroughfare.

沙海探油
Exploring for oil in a sea of sand.

塔里木绿洲中的棉山
A mountain of cotton in the Tarim oasis.

緑洲中的豐收景象 Bumper harvest in the oasis.

改造沙漠的引水工程 A diversion works project to transform the desert.

采摘新棉 Picking new cotton.

和田人在戈壁灘上修築引水干渠
Hotanese building channels on the
gobi to direct the flow of water.

豐收景象 Picture of a bumper harvest.

歌 舞 之 鄉 享 譽 天 下

　　塔里木盆地中的居民在久遠的歷史發展和絲綢之路的文化交往中，文化藝術活動形成了特殊的格調，成爲享譽國內外的歌舞之鄉。早在公元5、6世紀，當時龜茲(現今庫車)的音樂舞蹈家就到京都洛陽、長安傳播西域的音樂舞蹈藝術。到公元6世紀的盛唐時期，宮廷樂章中龜茲風格的舞樂更是自成一格，獨領風騷，成爲人們非常喜愛的音樂舞蹈。公元10世紀之后，《十二木卡姆》樂章的出現爲塔里木盆地的音樂舞蹈，乃至民間的歌舞曲藝注入了更大的活力，成爲流芳古今的著名樂章。由它構成的"喀什木卡姆"、"刀郎木卡姆"、"哈密木卡姆"、"吐魯番木卡姆"和"伊犁木卡姆"波及天山南北流傳至今。特別是其中的"喀什

木卡姆"其規模最大，形式多樣，共有170多首歌曲和器樂曲，72首間奏曲，演完這套"木卡姆"需要24小時。"木卡姆"演唱已經成爲流行于塔里木盆地大小綠洲中維吾爾族民間文化藝術的一種主要表現形式，每當節日、婚禮和喜慶以及貴客來臨，那激揚的樂曲、舒展的舞姿、優美的旋律都給人們帶來了無比的歡快，令每個參與者激動不已。今天在塔里木的綠洲中富有古老傳統和當代特色的民族歌舞更是五彩紛呈，使來自五湖四海的賓朋在領略异鄉异地的風情中感受那富有濃郁塔里木特色的藝術旋律。

節日里歡樂的人們　People celebrating a holiday.

果園里的歌舞 Sing and dancing in the orchard.

十二木卡姆演唱 A performance of "*The Twelve Mukkam.*"

HOME OF SONG AND DANCE ENJOY FAME THROUGHOUT THE WORLD

A unique style in culture and art has been formed by the residents of the Tarim Basin in their historical development influenced by the cultural exchange along the Silk Road, making it the home of song and dance, enjoying fame throughout the world. As early as in the 5th to 6th century, the musicians and dancers of Qiuci (today's Kuqa) had reached the then capital cities of Loyang and Changan to propagate their art. By the 6th century, during the heyday of the Tang Dynasty, Quici dance and music occupied an unchallenged position in court entertainment and became very popular among the people. After the10th century A. D. , "The Twelve Mukkam" composition appeared, injecting new life into the music and dance of the Tarim Basin and even into the folksongs, folk dances, and other folk musical entertainments, andbecame a musical work of lasting fame . The "Kashgar Mukkam", "The Dolang Mukkam", the "The Hami Mukkam ", "The Turpan Mukkam" andthe "Ili Mukkam" which grew from "The

Twelve Mukkam" reached both sides of the Tianshan Mountains and still remain popular to this day. Amongthem, "The Kashgar Mukkam" is the biggest is scale and most varied in form, with over 170 songs and instrumental performances, 72 refrains and takes about 24 hours to perform. Performing the "Mukkam" has become the main form of Uygur folk artistic cultural entertainment for those living in the big and small oases of the Tarim Basin. On high days and holidays, on weddings and other celebrations , and in welcoming guests, the invigorating music of the "Mukkam", the lively dance steps and rapid whirling of the dancers bring incomparable joy to the people and invigorating all the participants. In the oases of present–day Tarim where traditional characteristics are blended with modern ones , ethnic folk dances have have become all the more colorful, friends and guests from all over the world can experience the strong artistic rhythm of the Tarim in a highly exotic atmos phere.

刀郎麥西萊甫中的樂隊
The band in a Dolang meshrep.

維吾爾人喜歡"麥西萊甫"。這是一種又歌又舞的娛樂形式,流行于廣大的喀什噶爾綠洲各地。"麥西萊甫"歡快輕鬆,格調自由,男女老少均可參加。在主人宴請賓客時,這種娛樂還可增加飲宴間的熱烈氣氛。

The Uygurs are fond of the "Mexrep" which is an amusement form integrating songs with dances. It is popular all over the vast Kashgar Oasis. "Mexrep" is characterized by its relaxed and free steps. People of all ages, men and women, can take part in a "Mexrep". In particular, when entertaining guests, the "Mexrep" is an ideal amusement to add to the enthusiastic atmosphere of the party.

歌舞表演的民間老藝人 An old folk artists performing in song and dance.

雙人拔河
Tug – o' – war between two people.

雙人對舞 A dance for two people.

斗羊 Butting.

　　麥蓋提是刀朗舞之鄉,刀郎舞又在維吾爾舞蹈藝術中獨具風采。這種舞蹈的特點是具有廣泛的群衆性,跳起來情緒熱烈,狂放快樂,舞蹈中間夾雜的小品也詼諧風趣,令人捧腹,所以深受塔克拉瑪干邊緣各地刀朗人的歡迎。此舞大致分四個階段,中間插入許多小插曲,統稱"刀朗麥西萊甫"。莎車、巴楚、阿瓦提也比較流行。據説清代前后塔里木盆地南緣各地十分盛行這種舞蹈和娛樂活動,其歷史淵源十分久遠。

　　Markit is home of the Doran Dance. Doran dance has its unique style in the Uygur art of dancing . Its special characteristic lies in its popularity. The dance is enthusiastic and unrestrained . During the dance, skits and jokes are interspersed, which are very funny and make the audience roar with laughter. Therefore, the Doran dance is very popular among the Doran people who live on the edge of the Taklimakan. The Doran dance is roughly divided into four parts, with many short interludes. These interludes are generally called the " Doran Mexrep" the Doran dance is also rather popular in Shache, Bachu and Awati. It is said that around the Qing Dynasty, this dance was very popular in the southern part of the Tarim Basin. So its history is a very long one .

刀郎麥西萊甫
The Dolang meshrep.

如醉如痴的鼓手
Mesmerized drummers.

美麗的維吾爾族姑娘 Beautiful Uygur girl.

旅游探險方興未艾

作爲亞洲腹地的塔里木盆地，多年來是人們所注目所向往的地方。它的地理、民族、歷史文化和經濟生活繼19世紀一些國家的旅行探險家和考古工作者的光顧之后，近年來各種範圍的文化交往更加頻繁了。進入80年代，新疆維吾爾自治區每年接待20余萬人次的各國客人來到這片神奇誘人的盆地，走戈壁、進沙漠、訪綠洲、探古迹、登高原、逛集市，進行觀光考察、旅游探險，給他們留下了美好而難忘的記憶。

TOURISM AND EXPLORATION ON
THE BOOM

As the interior of the Asian Continent, the Tarim Basin has always been a focal point of interest for the people of the world. Especially since the 19th Century after the visits of the various archaeologists and explorers from the different countries in the world, its geographical location, its peoples, its historical culture and its economic life have further elicited warm interest from concerned circles throughout the world, and intellectual exchange have been greatly stepped up. Into the '80s, The Xinjiang Uygur Autonomous Region has received over 200,000 guests from different countries in the world to its magical and mystical Tarim Basin to see the Gobi and its deserts, to visit the oases, to explore its historical ruins, to ascend its highlands, and browse in its bazaars. These visits and surveys have left indelible marks on the fond memories of each guest.

法國探險隊徒步穿越塔克拉瑪干沙漠
French explorers crossing the Taklimakan Desert on foot.

考察古城　Investigating an ancient city.

考察隊在沙漠中與荒漠人家成了好鄰居
Investigators have become good neighbors with desert residents.

沙海探險中的駝隊　A caravan exploring the desert.
（刘玉生　摄）

旅游者在喀什 Tourists in Kashgar.

學術交流 Academic exchange.

科學考察 Scientific investigation.

乘滑翔機飛越沙海 Flying across the desert in a glider.

觀看文藝表演 Enjoying cultural entertainment.

中日學生聯合穿越死亡之海 (巴赫提亞 攝)
Joint adventure of Chinese and Japanese students crossing the 'sea of death'. (By Baktiyar)

行進到沙漠深處的駝隊 A caravan reaching the heart of the desert.

到達目的地 Arriving at the destination.

宿營地 Camping ground.

支援車隊 Relief convoy.

神秘的塔里木

编辑: 新疆對外文化交流協會
新疆人民出版社

出版: 新疆人民出版社

制版: 深圳軒風設計制版公司

印刷: 深圳寶峰印刷有限公司

260 × 250　12開本　13印張

1998年7月第一版　印數: 1—5000冊

ISBN 7-228-04707-9/J·215

定價: (平) 180元 (精) 220元